# British Social and Economic History Sources Coursework Questions

Simon Mason

Blackwell Education

## Acknowledgements

Bodleian Library 1B; Devon and Cornwall Record Society/Exeter University 3.3A; Mary Evans Picture Library Cover, Introduction A, 2.2B, 2.6L, 2.7D, 3.1E, 6.5D; Hampshire County Museum Service 1.10A; Hulton-Deutsch Collection 2.8B, 2.10F, 2.10G, 3.8F, 5.4C; Illustrated London News 2.6E, 2.6H, 3.6C, 5.3C; Mansell Collection 4.5A, 5.1B, 6.5B, 6.5C, 6.6B, 6.6C, 6.7B, 6.7C; Newcastle-upon-Tyne Teaching Archives 1.6A; Northumberland County Record Office 1.10C; Norwich Central Library 1.10B; Ordnance Survey 3.3B; Science Museum 1.8C, 2.5A, 2.5B; Somerset County Record Office 1.11F, 2.3B, 4.1A, 4.4B, 4.6A, 4.7A,B and C, 4.8A,B,C and D, 6.1A, 6.2B, 6.4B; Somerset Rural Life Museum 1.11G; St Bride's Printing Library 2.4A; Suffolk Record Office 1.8B; Thames TV 5.1A; Warwickshire Photographic Survey 1.7B, 1.7C; Welholme Galleries 7.1A; Welsh Folk Museum 1.10D.

The author and publishers are grateful to the following for permission to use material:

*The Agricultural Revolution 1750–1880*, J D Chambers & G E Mingay, B T Batsford Ltd; *An Illustrated History of Transport*, Anthony Ridley, William Heinemann; *Back to the Land: The Story of the W L A in Somerset*, Somerset Rural Life Museum; *Economic and Social History of England*, R B Jones, Longman UK Ltd; *Historic Railway Disasters* (Fourth Edition), O S Nock, revised by B K Cooper; Ian Allan Ltd; *The Industrial Revolution*, T S Ashton, Oxford University Press; *Industry and Empire*, E J Hobsbawm, George Weidenfeld & Nicolson Ltd; *The Machine Breakers*, Angela Bull, Collins; *The Making of the English Working Class*, E P Thompson, Victor Gollanz Ltd; *The Open Fields* by C S Orwin (Oxford University Press) 1938 use of map 1C.

The author would also like to thank Ms. Sue Berry for her help in finding material.

First published 1990
© Simon Mason 1990

Typeset by Photo·graphics, in 11/13 pt Palatino
Printed in Singapore by Kin Keong Printing Co. Pte. Ltd.

British Library Cataloguing in Publication Data
Mason, Simon
  British social and economic history: sources,
  coursework, revision for GCSE.
  1.  Great Britain. Social conditions, history
  I.  Title
  941

ISBN 0-631-90152-3

# Contents

# Teacher's introduction

Many teachers of GCSE courses have been searching for useful and interesting primary and secondary sources which they can use either as back-up material for lessons or as instruments for GCSE course-work. The source material in this book has been specifically chosen for teachers and pupils involved in GCSE Social and Economic History.

The source material has been adapted and edited in such a way as to make it accessible to pupils of all levels of ability. There is a wealth of absorbing evidence including formal and informal documents, statistics, maps and charts, drawings and photographs, plays and poems. There are extended questions designed to help students interpret the evidence and to make deductions and comparisons. There are also case studies, quizzes and games. None of these sources has appeared in other history textbooks.

The layout of the book loosely follows the pattern laid down in the Blackwell History Project: Agriculture; Industry; Transport; Social Change. Primary and secondary sources are followed by questions which are intended to test a student's understanding of historical evidence, concepts and skills. I have not attempted to include mark schemes. These are best left to colleagues whose awareness of their own pupils' individual needs and intellectual strengths will always be greater than that of any examiner or author. If any colleague would like further advice or clarification of any issues raised by the sources, I can be contacted via the publishers.

Simon Mason

# Pupil's introduction

**A** Accident on the Hampstead Junction railway, 1861

Source **A** is a piece of historical evidence. It shows an accident on the Hampstead Junction railway in 1861.

A major part of an historian's job is asking questions about the past. Make a list of the questions you would want to ask about **A** if you were writing a book about transport in the nineteenth century. You should think about *who* drew the picture, *why* it was drawn and *what* impact the picture had on people who saw it.

Now look at the picture again. How do you think the accident happened? Why are there so many people standing around? Can we be sure that this accident really happened? After all, the artist could have made it up!

On its own, **A** is difficult to understand. It is like one piece in a very large jigsaw. If you can find the other pieces of the jigsaw, the source makes more sense.

The other pieces of the historian's jigsaw could take the form of maps, graphs, histograms, engravings, photographs, letters . . . the list is endless. Sometimes you find that pieces of the jigsaw are missing!

One feature of the GCSE History courses is the use and understanding of sources in classroom teaching, coursework assignments and examination papers. The aim of this book is to help you to answer *source-based* questions. The book is divided up into six sections. Each section provides sources on a particular topic. In most cases, GCSE-type questions follow the sources. You can work through the sections in any order. However, the questions in the first section, 'Agriculture', are slightly easier than the questions in the final section, 'Social Change'. If possible, you should refer to some of the other History textbooks mentioned in the bibliography at the end of the book. In the questions requiring longer answers you should include as much information as possible.

Most students enjoy working with sources. They say they like working individually or in groups on 'real' history assignments. They know they can apply the skills they learn in History to other academic subjects and to work they do outside school.

Steps 1–5 below give you a specific plan for evaluating historical sources. Use this method whenever possible in your GCSE work.

1 Read through the source material. Make a list of any words or phrases you don't understand. Then look them up in a dictionary. Once you have understood the meaning of all of the words, the meaning of the passage should become clearer. If you are unable to look the word up, a good tip is mentally to remove the word or phrase you don't understand from the passage. Then substitute another word which helps the sentence to make sense. A substituted word is called a *synonym* (word with a similar meaning) and will often have the same meaning as the word you have removed.

2 Decide what type of evidence is in front of you. Is it a drawing, a photo, a document, a map, a report, a poem or a passage from a novel?

3 Are there any clues as to the date of the evidence?

4 Is the source *primary* (produced at the time the event happened) or *secondary* (produced some time after the event happened)?

5 How *reliable* is the evidence? Is there any reason for doubting its accuracy?

This technique can be summarised as follows: 1 Meanings; 2 Type; 3 Date; 4 Primary or secondary; 5 Reliability.

Now apply steps 1–5 to **B**. See how much you can find out about it!

❜*The crowd began to assemble at 4 am and when the sun rose it shone upon the most motley collection of people brought together beneath the gallows of Exeter. Some had travelled great distances on the railway to attend the execution. At seven minutes past eight o'clock the head of Calcraft appeared above the turret of the gallows. A murmur, then a shout, spread through every part of the crowd. The adjustment of the rope to the top beam of the gallows was the work of nearly three minutes; and just as Calcraft descended from the steps, the culprit appeared upon the platform, carried in a chair by the warders. She was wearing the dress she had worn at her trial and her hair was bound up tightly to her temples and brought into a twist at the back. She seemed to be perfectly helpless but conscious till she gazed upon the scene stretching out before her. This was evidently too much for her and her head drooped, apparently in a swoon. When the executioner twisted the rope around her neck, she slightly raised her head and opened her eyes with a wide stare of helplessness and hopelessness. The white cap was drawn over her face, the chair on which she had been sitting was withdrawn, and she was lifted upright into a standing posture supported by three warders. Her head drooped upon her breast, and in this position she was held for over three minutes, whilst Calcraft tied the end of the rope with a succession of tight knots.*

*The drop was over laid by two or three strong boards stretched across the gallows; and on these boards two warders stepped above the culprit when Calcraft stepped aside to carry out his dreadful duty. A minute's horrible suspense followed. At a signal from Calcraft, the men dropped the body; the crash and thud of the drop broke the dead silence which reigned in every part of the crowd; and the culprit fell through the orifice. A frightful scene followed. Bound hand and foot as she was, the woman manifested a strange strength and nerve. Instead of dying in a swoon, she was manifestly perfectly conscious of her position; and the instant after she fell, she swung herself round and grasped at the plank stretched across the gallows. This was instantly withdrawn but still the convict struggled in mid air. Her neck had not been broken and Calcraft took her by the legs from below and ended her sufferings by pulling her body downwards with his utmost strength. She still seemed to live for a moment, raising her hands slightly – but in another second was still. The poisoner of her husband was dead.*❜ **(B)**

(*Trewman's Exeter Flying Post*, March 28 1866)

# Questions

**1** What is meant by: gallows; swoon; manifested?

**2** In which newspaper was **B** first published?

**3** Was **B** written in the eighteenth, nineteenth or twentieth century?

**4** Is **B** a primary or secondary source?

**5** How reliable is **B**? Why was it published?

By now you should have some ideas about the nature of the source and its accuracy and reliability. We now need to look at some *speculative* questions (questions open to argument). You will probably come across these in coursework and exams. Often you will be asked what you think about a source. It does not matter a great deal what opinion you give in your answer as long as your writing is supported by firm evidence from the source itself.

**6** Why do you think 'the culprit' was carried to her execution on a chair?

**7** What was the writer's attitude to: **a** Calcraft; **b** 'the culprit'; **c** the crowd?

**8** Why was it necessary for Calcraft to pull the legs of the criminal?

**9** How could the extract be used as an argument *against* capital punishment?

# Section I
# AGRICULTURE

# 1 History detective: open field farming

Four pieces of historical evidence about open field farming have come into your hands, sources **A**, **B**, **C** and **D**.

To play History Detective, follow the steps below carefully.

**1** Look through the four pieces of evidence on your own. In your rough book or on scrap paper, jot down any ideas which occur to you as you read through the evidence.

**2** Divide yourselves into groups and discuss the evidence.

    **a**   Are there any words you don't understand?

    **b**   What different types of evidence are **A–D**?

    **c**   Is there anything strange or unusual about the evidence?

    **d**   What does the evidence tell you about open field farming?

    **e**   How has farming changed since the seventeenth century in this village?

    **f**   What is unusual about Laxton?

    **g**   Who might have written or drawn the evidence?

    **h**   Are sources **A** to **D** pieces of primary or secondary evidence?

    **i**   What is the date of each piece of evidence?

    **j**   How reliable is each piece of evidence?

    **k**   What other questions do you want to ask about the evidence?

**3** In your groups write a 200-word report on the evidence you have in front of you. Make sure all the facts in your report are correct. Later on you will have to explain the comments you have made

# RULES AND REGULATIONS FOR THE GRAZING OF THE OPEN FIELDS

**1** The Open Fields are to be grazed by those tenants of the Minister of Agriculture, Fisheries and Food and Earl Manvers who cultivate land in the Open Fields.

**2** A tenant who has no unenclosed land is not allowed to turn any stock into the Fields.

**3** A tenant, whose holding does not exceed a total of 40 acres, may turn stock into the Fields under these rules and regulations, though he may not have unenclosed land in *each* of the three Fields. Tenants holding over 40 acres can only turn stock into the Fields in which they have unenclosed land.

**4** The Fields are to be stocked as follows:
(a) THE WHEAT FIELD – unlimited stock from the breaking up of the Field to the 20th October in the same year or such earlier date as the three Foremen decide.
(b) THE BEAN AND CLOVER FIELD – unlimited stock from the breaking up of the Field to the 23rd November in the same year.
(c) THE FALLOW FIELD – from the 23rd November in one year to the 8th October in the following year, twenty sheep by each tenant. No cattle or horses are allowed in this Field during this period.

**5** All stock must be the personal property of the tenant and no joint stock are to be allowed under any circumstances. Anyone transgressing this rule will be liable to be fined by the Jury.

**6** No sheep are to be turned into an Open Field until they have been properly dressed, such dressing to be done before they are turned in.

**7** No tup is to be turned into the Fields before the 15th October, or to remain there later than the 23rd December in any year.

**8** The Foreman of the Juries and the Parish Pinder are to see that these rules are carried out and are immediately to report anyone breaking them to the Minister's Agents, and anyone so reported may, after one caution, be given notice to quit his Farm.

The Commission appeal to the Minister's tenants, in their common interests, to help him and the Foreman of the Juries to carry out these rules. Tenants are asked specially to be careful to shut the gates on the Commons when passing through them and also the gates on the lands which have been inclosed.

Agricultural Land Commission
April 1959.

**A** Agricultural regulations, Laxton, 1959

about the sources. Your report should be written as clearly as possible. Make sure it is legible. At the end of your report, explain why you think the sources are primary or secondary.

**4** Appoint a spokesperson for your group. Each group will take it in turns to read out its report. No changes can be made to the written report. Any member of any other group can challenge facts in your report by putting up their hand and saying 'Challenge!' A successful challenge will give your group one minus point. The winning group is the group with the least number of minus points at the end of the lesson.

**B**  Map of Laxton

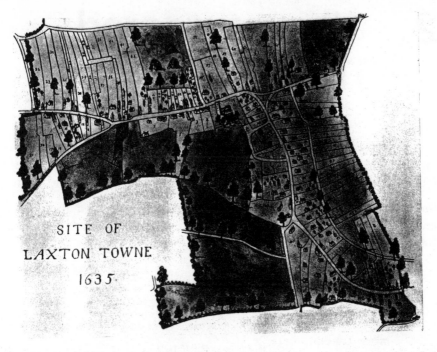

SITE OF
LAXTON TOWNE
1635.

**C** Laxton – the last open field village

| | 1625 | | BEFORE RE-ORGANIZATION IN 1904 | |
|---|---|---|---|---|
| West (and East) Field | 444 acres in | 617 strips | 217 acres in | 264 strips |
| Mill Field | 433 acres in | 798 strips | 294 acres in | 410 strips |
| South Field | 428 acres in | 746 strips | 269 acres in | 398 strips |
| | 1305 | 2161 | 780 | 1072 |
| Total | | | | |

| AFTER RE-ORGANIZATION | | |
|---|---|---|
| West Field | 156 acres in | 65 strips |
| Mill Field | 209 acres in | 97 strips |
| South Field | 169 acres in | 78 strips |
| Total | 534 | 240 |

| TODAY | | | |
|---|---|---|---|
| West Field | 146 acres in | 50 strips | 23 acres in sykes |
| Mill Field | 196 acres in | 68 strips | 24 acres in sykes (sykes = water |
| South Field | 141 acres in | 47 strips | 38 acres in sykes          meadows) |
| Total | 483 | 165 | 85 |

**D** Farming statistics, Laxton

# 2 Who murdered Thomas Carter?

At 6.30 am on 5 May 1796, the dead body of Thomas Carter, a poor farmer, was found on the outskirts of the village of Brympton Turville (see map **A** below). Thomas Carter had been shot through the neck.

Sort through the 26 pieces of information in the information file (**B**) and study the map carefully. You should be able to work out what happened to Thomas Carter on the night of 4 May 1796. Explain how you have arrived at your conclusions.

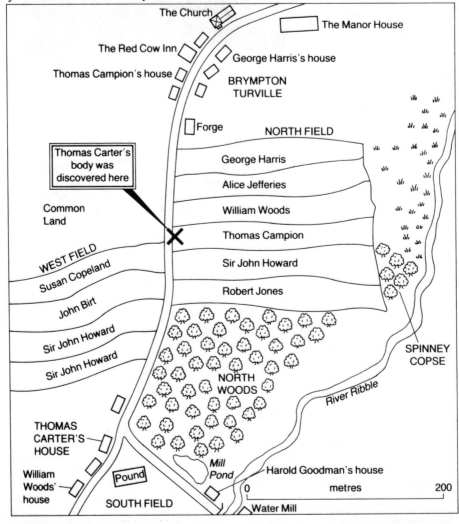

**A** Map of Brympton Turville

1 Thomas Carter left the Red Cow Inn at 11.30 pm on 4 May.

2 Thomas Carter had been unemployed since 6 March, 1796. He had a wife and three children to support.

3 The local Squire, Sir John Howard, had publicly announced that anyone caught poaching deer or rabbits on his land would 'receive the full measure of the law'.

4 John Chapman, the miller, had borrowed a hunting rifle from Sir John Howard on 3 May, 1796.

5 At about 11.35 pm on May 4, 1796, a shot was heard coming from Spinney Copse in North Field.

6 William Woods had been seen shooting at crows at dusk on 4 May, 1796.

7 At 7.30 pm on 4 May, 1796, Thomas Carter was seen drinking in the Red Cow Inn.

8 Harold Smith was a very heavy drinker. On the night of 4 May, 1796, he consumed 12 pints of cider.

9 Robert Jones had been seen in the company of John Birt's wife.

10 William Woods owned one strip in North Field, no strips in West Field and 13 strips in South Field.

11 Alice Jefferies hated Susannah Carter because of a disagreement over some ducks on mill pond.

12 Thomas Carter had quarrelled with Harold Smith, the village blacksmith over the payment of drinks in the Red Cow Inn on 25 April, 1796. The argument had nearly come to blows.

13 Sir John Howard's wife, Lady Margaret, was very concerned about the welfare of village children.

14 Harold Goodman had been suspected of poaching deer in 1795. No firm evidence had been brought against him.

15 William Woods believed that his wife, Susan, had been bewitched by Alice Jefferies.

16 Thomas Carter had been very friendly with a widow, Alice Jefferies. Some people believed he had been too friendly with her!

17 William Woods owned a rusty old musket which had belonged to his grandfather.

18 Robert Jones had a violent temper.

19 A roe deer was found caught up in the undergrowth in North Woods on the morning of 5 May, 1796. A bullet had grazed its back.

20 After a dispute over boundaries, John Birt had been abusive to Susan Copeland.

21 Thomas Campion had always been fond of Thomas Carter's wife, Susannah. He had courted her before she was married to Thomas.

22 William Woods had quarrelled with Alice Jefferies over weeds spreading across his strip in North Field.

23 Sir John Howard, the squire, owned one strip in North Field, two strips in West Field and 29 strips in South Field.

24 Harold Goodman was in possession of firearms on the night of 4 May, 1796.

25 A roe deer was seen running across North Field at about 11.40 pm on 4 May, 1796.

26 Two farm workers, George Harris and Harold Goodman were drinking in the Red Cow Inn on the night of 4 May, 1796. They left at 10.45 pm.

**B** Information file

# 3 The changing village 1752–1882

Sources **A–G** provide information about enclosures in the late eighteenth century. Aston Blank is a village in Gloucestershire. In 1752 the village contained 40 houses and had a population of 171. All the houses were in the centre of the village (see **A**). The area of the open fields surrounding the village was 1 600 acres, divided up into half-acre strips. There were 140 acres of commons and 253 acres of enclosed land. **B** shows how the village changed after enclosure when there were only seven landowners. The other sources in this section reveal how and why these changes took place.

**A**  Pre-enclosure map of Aston Blank, Gloucester, 1752

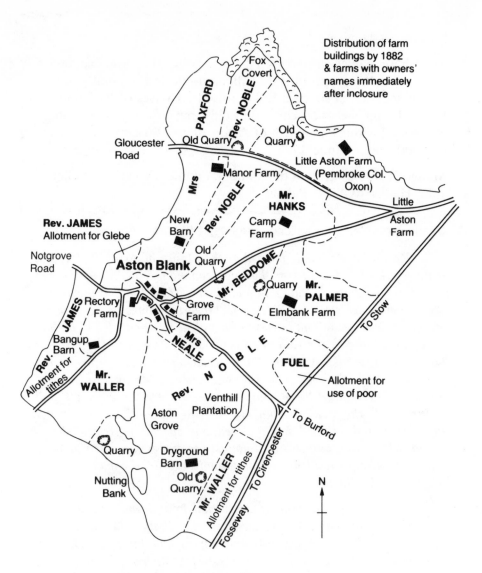

Distribution of farm
buildings by 1882
& farms with owners'
names immediately
after inclosure

Fox
Covert

PAXFORD

Rev. NOBLE

Gloucester
Road

Old Quarry

Old
Quarry

Little Aston Farm
(Pembroke Col.
Oxon)

Mrs NOBLE

Manor Farm

Mr.
HANKS

Little

Rev. JAMES
Allotment for Glebe

New
Barn

Camp
Farm

Aston
Farm

Notgrove
Road

Old
Quarry

Aston Blank

Mr. BEDDOME

Quarry

Mr.
PALMER

Rectory
Farm

Grove
Farm

Elmbank Farm

To Stow

JAMES

Bangup
Barn

Mrs
NEALE

N
O
B
L
E

FUEL

Rev.
Allotment for
tithes

Mr.
WALLER

Rev.

Venthill
Plantation

Allotment for
use of poor

Aston
Grove

To Burford

Quarry

Dryground
Barn

To Cirencester

Nutting
Bank

Old
Quarry

Mr. WALLER

Allotment for tithes

Fosseway

N

**B**   Post-enclosure map of Aston Blank, 1882

In 1794 the Reverend Mungo Noble married the daughter of the
Bishop of Waterford. The Bishop gave the manor of Aston Blank to
the Reverend Noble as part of his daughter's dowry (marriage gift).
In return, the Bishop demanded a rent of £276 a year for the manor.
This was asking a lot as the profit on the Bishop's 1 106 acres was
only £275 a year! To make more money from his land, the Reverend
Noble applied to Parliament for an Enclosure Act (**C**).

Mr Robert Hughes,

We whose names are written below, being the principal proprietors, in the parish of Aston Blank do hereby appoint you to be our solicitor to solicit a Bill before the Houses of Parliament for enclosing the open common fields, meadows, pastures and waste land within the parish of Aston Blank. Witness our hands this 30th day of June 1794.

Mungo H Noble (Lord of the Manor), F James (Vicar), E Waller, John Hanks, William Palmer.

**C** Landowners' letter to solicitor Hughes, 1794

❢ *The Reverend Mr Noble is Lord of the Manor of Aston Blank, and owner of the greater part of the open common fields, meadows and pastures . . . Edmund Waller is owner of certain lands lying in the said common fields . . . the Reverend Frederick James is vicar of the church of Cold Aston and in right of his vicarage is entitled to certain glebe lands lying in the said open common fields and to the tythe of hay . . . John Hanks, William Palmer and various other people are owners of the other parts of the said open fields and unenclosed lands . . . These lands lie in small parcels and are therefore difficult to farm. All the owners want to see the open fields and other unenclosed lands divided and enclosed, and specific parts and shares rented out, set out, and shared amongst the owners . . . such division will greatly help the farmers, yet cannot be properly made without the help of Parliament.*

*May it therefore please your Majesty that John Stame of Pull Court in the County of Worcester, gentleman, John Chamberlain of Cropreadly in the County of Oxford, gentleman, and John Craddock of Northleach in the County of Gloucester, gentleman, be appointed commissioners for the purposes of dividing, setting out and allotting the said open common fields, meadows, pastures and downs in Aston Blank . . . and it is declared that each of them will be paid the sum of two pounds and two shillings per day for their trouble and expenses, and no more, for themselves, their horses, their servants . . .*

*Each commissioner shall take this oath: 'I do swear that I will faithfully, fairly and honestly, according to the best of my skill and judgement, carry out the commission entrusted to me.'*

*And whereas fuel is scarce in the parish of Aston Blank, the owners of the land are willing to supply the poor with wood and furze (dry gorse).* ❢  **(D)**

(Bill for dividing and enclosing the open fields of Aston Blank, 1795)

❛ *May 12–16, 1795. The commissioners met on the 12th and on the following three days they valued the land to be divided and enclosed and also all the old enclosures within the parish, and ordered Mr Clarke, the surveyor, to make a book thereof.*

*On the 16th they set out the public roads over the lands to be divided and enclosed.*

*Ordered . . . that an advert be placed in the Gloucester Journal on Monday 25 May and Monday 1 June:*

*ASTON BLANK ENCLOSURES. We the commissioners appointed by an Act of Parliament for dividing and enclosing the open common fields, meadows, pastures and downs hereby give notice that all landowners do send or deliver in to Mr Henry Clarke, the surveyor, at the Coach and Horses in Burton on the Water, all their respective claims on the open common fields, pastures and downs. And also to send on a separate piece of paper, sealed up, a description in writing of the situation in which they want their new allotments to be placed . . .* ❜  (E)

(Commissioners' Minute Book, 1795)

**Expenses**

| | |
|---|---|
| Reverend Mungo Henry Noble | £1 121 |
| John Hanks | £ 355 |
| Edmund Waller, Edward Frier | £ 170 |
| Mrs Mary Neale | £ 33 |
| Thomas Hutchman | £ 1 |
| Owner of Little Ashton Farm | £ 30 |
| Reverend Mr James | £ 10 |
| William Palmer, George Draper | £ 286 |
| Mrs Paxford | £ 302 |
| Total | £2 308 |

(These expenses to cover the cost of obtaining the Act; solicitors', commissioners', surveyors' fees; fencing the allotments; making the public roads; for hedges; for cloverseed sown in the allotments.)

**F** List of expenses from the Commissioners' Minute Book

**Before enclosure**
*Income*
Rent                                                £ 275
Rent from other estates                             £ 171
Deduct the Bishop's rent                            £ 276

Therefore to pay the steward's salary and
carry out repairs, Mr Noble had only            _____
                                                    £ 170
                                                _____

**After enclosure**
*Income*
Rent                                                £ 852
Deduct the Bishop's rent                            £ 276
                                                _____
    Total income                                    £ 576
                                                _____

**G**   Variation of rental of the Reverend Mr Noble's estate before and after enclosure, 1798

# Questions

**1** Describe how and why the village of Aston Blank was enclosed in the late eighteenth century. How would life in the village be different after enclosure? (You should write a long answer to this. Use sources **A–G** in your answer.)

**2** The following quotations come from well-known GCSE History books. Does the evidence in sources **A–G** support or contradict these statements? Explain your answers.
   **a** 'Each open field village was surrounded by three large, unfenced fields.'
   **b** 'The poor always suffered as a result of enclosures.'
   **c** 'The main reason for making enclosures was money.'
   **d** 'Each strip in an open field was one acre in area.'
   **e** 'Parliament was unsympathetic towards the plight of the poor.'
   **f** 'Poor people had no warning that an enclosure was about to take place.'
   **g** 'Only the wealthiest landowners could afford the cost of enclosure.'

**3** You have been asked to write an essay about parliamentary enclosure in the eighteenth century. Do you think sources **A–G** provide you with enough information to write the essay? Give reasons for your answer.

# 4 The enclosure game

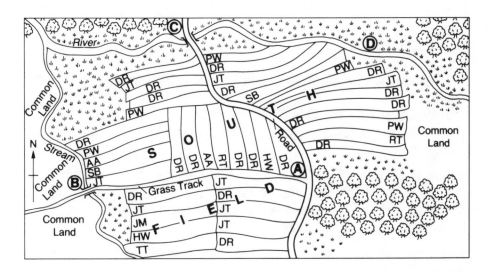

Look at the map. It shows part of the Midlands in the 1750s. A wealthy landowner, the Duke of Romsley, has decided to build ten farm workers' cottages, a pub and a church on his estate.

## Questions

**1** Which of the sites **A–D** on the map do you think would be best? The Duke has to bear in mind that the cottages need to be: **a** near a common; **b** near the road; **c** near the wood; **d** near the strips (fields); **e** near the stream/river.

**2** Why do you think it was important for people's homes to be near these places?

**3** Draw a chart like the one below. Give each site **A–D** a mark out of ten according to how many points you think it is worth. For example, if you think site **A** is a long way from the wood, give it two or three out of ten for **c** (see above).

| | Site A | | Site B | | Site C | | Site D | |
|---|---|---|---|---|---|---|---|---|
| | own result | class result | own result | class result | own result | class result | own result | class result |
| **a** | | | | | | | | |
| **b** | | | | | | | | |
| **c** | | | | | | | | |
| **d** | | | | | | | | |
| **e** | | | | | | | | |
| Totals | | | | | | | | |

**4 a** Which site do you think is best? What advice would you give the Duke?

**b** Which site do the class think is best?

**c** Mark in the ten cottages, church and pub on your map at your chosen site.

**5** Five years pass. The Duke decides to turn the strips in South Field into patchwork fields. He tries to be fair about this. He has to bear in mind that each of his tenant farmers is entitled to a certain amount of land. Look again at the map.

How many strips do the following farmers and villagers own in South Field? (See key.)

| Name | Initials on map | No. of strips |
|---|---|---|
| The Duke of Romsley | DR | |
| Mr Trelawney | JT | |
| Parson Williams | PW | |
| Ann Ayre | AA | |
| Susannah Barrett | SB | |
| Robert Tucker | RT | |
| Jethro Mayne | JM | |
| Harold Webber | HW | |
| Timothy Towers | TT | |

**6** You are the Duke's surveyor. It is your job to redraw the map of South Field so that compact fields are created which can be fenced, ditched and drained.

When re-drawing the map of South Field, you need to bear in mind the following points:

**(i)** Assume that the area of each strip is one acre.

**(ii)** The farmers should have their newly-created fields as close to each other as possible and/or linked by the road. The fields must not be scattered all over the place.

**(iii)** The woods, the marshy ground and the land to the west (left) of the stream and the common land are not to be enclosed.

**(iv)** There will be no need to cut across existing strips.

When you have decided how to enclose South Field, mark in the borders of your new 'patchwork' fields. Then mark in the new owners (use colours and a key if you like). Check that each farmer has the amount of land he or she is entitled to.

**7** Answer these questions by studying your new map of South Field.

  **a** Who seems to have gained most from the enclosure?

  **b** Who seems to have 'lost out'?

  **c** You are charging very high fees for carrying out the survey. What might happen to poor farmers who are unable to pay your fees?

  **d** How might the changes you have made affect the life of the villagers?

  **e** What difficulties did you face when re-drawing the map of the village?

  **f** Where might new farms appear? Mark them on the map.

  **g** Where would you build new roads? Mark them on your map.

# 5 The Board of Agriculture Survey

In 1794 the Board of Agriculture produced a report on the agriculture of each county in England. The Board sent out questionnaires to farmers all over the country. The eleven answers given in **A** were written by a farm bailiff in the north-east of England.

Study the source material carefully.

Answers to the Queries (published and set forth by the Board of Agriculture; as far as they relate to an Estate belonging to the Right Honorable Lord Delaval; situate at Ford in the Parish of Ford and County of Northumberland.

Answer to }
Query 1st } — The nature of the soil of this Estate is composed principally of a light loamy soil; together with various tenements of the greatest ease in which manage a farm — employed with clay; accordingly to perhaps the growth of Turnips; situate in the moist nation. Tracts of that part of great Britain called Loyal.

Do. 2d — Possessed by one Proprietor only.

Do. 3d — Occupied by both great and small Farmers.

Do. 4th — The Lands in this Estate is employed both in Husbandry and Pasture.

Do. 5th — The Grasses cultivated are Rice and White Clover, Rye Grass; are mostly the common Hay &c. The Roses are principally of the several kinds; or bred by the Farmers from a Cross of the strong English Stallion and Scotch Mare; which stock produces very good Horses for Draught.
The horned Cattle consists of the Dutch bred & Scots growth; brought here and by & by grazing great attention in procuring some of the best milch cows. This differs
The sheep are principally of the most approved old

Answer to }
Query 6th — The watering of Lands not attempt always, temporary practicable, as those are only now particular places capable. I was going that Mode of managing of goods Lands.

Do. 7th — Grains generally cultivated are Herbarts in tillage are Wheat, Rye, Barley, Oats, Pease, Beans &c. Quantity of Beans.

Do. 8th — The Rotation of Crops are first the long fallow; when first plowed and sort of Oats, then Wheat; that after wrought in the spring for Barley; not followed by Turnips and green Turnips with; sleeve & cows with wheat or Barley; sow sometimes with Oats or Rye; if the Laws of Mr. Grass; sown of milk Clover and Rye Grass; or they seeds; the Green Crops such as Turnips and Clover are grown here in the greatest Perfection.

Do. 9th — The whole of the Lands is in Husbandry and Tillage; as the Quantities seem in Rotation; each of Turnips or Wheat; but principally of a Turnip.

Do. 10th — Manures used are Lime, Chalk and Sea Dung; and sometimes Compost.

Do. 11th — The implements of Husbandry are the best improved the Ford Plough; with a no less accommodate by the late improved Scotch Cart, distinguished in various experimental Husbandry; the most approved old. Together with the ——

# Questions

**1** Write out the answers to queries (questions) 1–5 in your own hand-writing. This is called *transcribing* material.

**2** Who owned the estate and what was its name?

**3** In which parish and county was the estate?

**4** Who was Cuthbert Clark?

**5** Match up the questions below with the answers in the source material. They are the questions sent out by the Board in the wrong order. For example, query 3 in the source material is the answer to **a** below.
  **a**  Are the farms small or great?
  **b**  How many people own the land?
  **c**  What grasses are cultivated and what sort of farm stock is kept?
  **d**  Is any of the land watered?
  **e**  What sort of ploughs and carts are used?
  **f**  Are there fallow fields?
  **g**  What is the nature of the soil and climate in the neighbourhood?
  **h**  Is the land employed for pasture or arable purposes, or a mixture of both?
  **j**  What manures are made use of?
  **k**  What grains are cultivated?
  **l**  What is the rotation of crops?

**6** Draw a table like the one below to show the type of crop rotation used in this part of the country between 1789 and 1794. It was a six-course Northumberland rotation, so you will need six fields on your diagram:

|          | 1    | 2     | 3       | 4      | 5     | 6      |
|----------|------|-------|---------|--------|-------|--------|
| 1789     | Oats | Wheat | Turnips | Barley | Grass | Clover |
| 1790     |      |       |         |        |       |        |
| 1791 etc |      |       |         |        |       |        |

**7** Why do you think the Board of Agriculture sent out the questionnaire? How might the questionnaire have helped farmers to improve their crop yields?

# 6 Rastrick's threshing machine

Threshing (or thrashing) corn involves separating the ears of grain from the 'chaff' (straw). For thousands of years farm workers had carried out this operation using a flail, a wooden staff with a heavy stick attached to it. In the late eighteenth century, a number of farmers and inventors produced threshing machines for use on farms. These were supposed to thresh large quantities of corn much more quickly than the old flails. One of these farmers was John Rastrick of Morpeth, Northumberland. **A** is a plan and description of his threshing machine. The machine is fairly simple and the way it works is explained in the reference key at the side of the diagram. The semi-octagonal or round buildings built to shelter the machinery were known locally as 'gin-gans'. You can still see them on many Northumberland farms.

## Questions

**1** What is meant by 'threshing' or 'thrashing' corn?

**2** Make a list in your own words of what letters **A–I** on the diagram stand for.

**3** How was the threshing machine powered?

**4** Did the wheel which supplied the power to the machine sit vertically or horizontally?

**5** How many sheaves of corn could be threshed in six hours?

**6** What might have been the drawbacks of using a machine like this in the 1780s? You should think about: mechanical problems; bad weather; soil types; conservatism (fear of change); maintenance.

**7** What other sources of power might have been available on Northumberland farms in 1780?

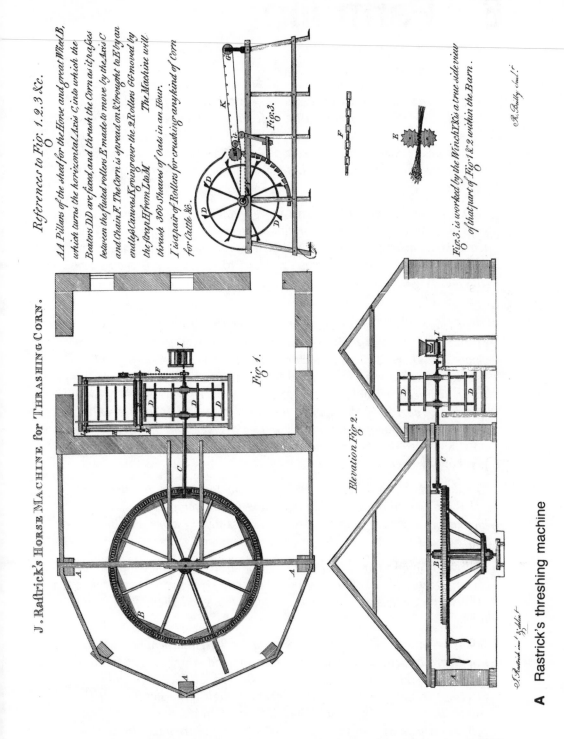

J. Rastrick's HORSE MACHINE for THRASHING CORN.

*References to Fig: 1. 2. 3 &c.*

A A Pillars of the shed for the Horse and great Wheel B, which turns the horizontal Axis C, into which the Beaters D D are fixed, and thrash the Corn as it passes between the fluted rollers E made to move by the Axis C and Chain F. The Corn is spread on & brought to E by an end less Canvas Kr ing over the 2 Rollers GG moved by the ferw H F from L to M      The Machine will thrash 360 Sheaves of Oats in an Hour.

I is a pair of Rollers for crushing any kind of Corn for Cattle &c.

Fig: 3.

Fig. 1.

Elevation Fig: 2.

Fig.3. is worked by the Winch I R is a true side view of that part of Fig: 1 & 2 within the Barn.

A  Rastrick's threshing machine

**8** How would most threshing machines have been powered by 1850?

# 7 Farm life

❝Unless the farm labourer starts his education early, and learns in the fields, he will learn very little. The young labourer is taken from school as soon as he can earn 4d or 6d (2p or 2½p) on the farm. He forgets all he has learned at school as fast as boys do, and can do little more than just retain what he was taught before he was ten years of age.

As he grows bigger, he is worth more money. He leaves home and goes into service as a mate or lad to help the waggoner with the team. He boards with a respectable waggoner, whose wife takes care of his clothes etc. But he is soon anxious to marry and is seen some fine morning before he is 22, on his way from church, with his bride who is 17 . . .

They lodge themselves in a couple of furnished rooms in a noisy row of cottages. They hire the furniture off a broker and all goes on smoothly. There is plenty of work, she is a good housewife, and by the time there are a couple of children, they are in a cottage. One thing has been a trouble and that is the broker's bill. As the dealer saw his opportunity, he would sell them pieces of furniture which they had previously rented. So, by slow degrees, the bed they sleep on, the table, the chairs, the clock are their own. Still, they have not bought cheap.

The doctor's bill is a heavy item but the doctor is kind and will wait till they can pay him . . . In addition is the monthly call of the bagman-clothier for the payment on a dress nearly worn out, but not nearly paid for; also of the bagman shoemaker . . .

There is also another child on the way and this time the couple have fewer scruples about obtaining Poor Law relief, for the ice was broken on a former occasion; and if their case was good then, it is better now.

In the meantime the husband has joined a sick and benefit club. He had heard of several which offered various advantages, but nothing so good he thinks as the Black Bear Benefit Club, which holds its meetings in the pub every other Saturday night. The landlord of the 'Black Bear' runs the club. The club night gives the husband the opportunity to spend an hour or two with his friends. His wife is pleased with his account of his evening's amusement – and he never *comes home the worse for drink, rather the better. And if the first Monday in May is fine the annual club party has attractions for both husband and wife. The one has a dinner and tobacco, the other lemonade, wine, cakes, almonds and nuts. The dance which winds up the party is enjoyed by one and all.*

*The cottage he lives in is not so bad but the rent is high – 3s (15p) a week. He might get a hovel for 1s (5p) and a very cheap tenement for 2s 6d (12½p). He takes in a lodger or two but with an increasing family and extra work for his wife, things get rather difficult. Still, they are a respectable couple and that at a time when there are many mouths to feed, and no child yet old enough to earn as much as 4d (2p) a day on the farm. The children go to school, on Sundays, and to church as well; and the mother is glad to get them out of the way morning and afternoon. Both parents go in the afternoon to church.*

*And thus time passes on, and sees the family of six or seven children; the oldest boy working like a man at a shilling a day, and eating like two men; and the second, only nine years old, occasionally employed in seed time as a walking scarecrow; at other times as a sheep-boy at 6d a day. Here are the average earnings of the family for a week and their expenses.*

| Income | | | Expenses | | |
|---|---|---|---|---|---|
| | *s* | *d* | | *s* | *d* |
| *Father (average)* | 14 | – | House-rent | 3 | – |
| *Mother (average)* | 2 | – | Club | | 9 |
| *Eldest boy (average)* | 7 | – | Food (8 in family) | 15 | 6 |
| *Second boy (average)* | 2 | – | Beer (at home) at 1s 4d a gallon | 1 | – |
| | | | Schooling for 3 children | | 6 |
| | | | Fuel | 2 | – |
| *Total* | 25s | | *Total* | 22s | 9d |

*There remains a balance of 2s 3d for the bagman and for clothing father, mother and children, for bedding, for accidents and repairs to furniture and other expenses.*

*If the couple are blessed with health and strength, and cheerful tempers, they continue to struggle on. But no man can count on a single day's good health. Illness comes at times – now look at the dark side of the picture.*

| Income | |
|---|---|
| **Income** | |
| Father ill – on the club | 10s |
| Mother's average (work in the fields) | 2s |
| Boys' average | 9s |
| | 21s |
| From Union, four children dependent on medical relief | 4s |
| Total | 25s |

Pass on six years and look at the farm labourer again. He has been married over 20 years, and the family are growing up. Two sons, out as lodgers, are conducting themselves on the 'approved system' as their father before them; two daughters out at service, one boy at 7s a week; one girl still at school.

| Earnings | | Expenses | |
|---|---|---|---|
| Father | 14s | Rent | 3s – |
| Mother | 2s | Club | 9d |
| Boy | 7s | Beer | 1s – |
| Total | | Food | 9s – |
| | 23s | Schooling | 3d |
| | | Fuel | 2s – |
| | | Total | 16s |

It will be seen that in the former period there remained 2s 3d for clothes and other outgoings; now there is 7s and the parents find things easier.

The age of the husband is now about 43 in years and 53 in condition. He is, however, a good worker and a steady, honest man. But he might now begin to save money, and has heard a great deal about savings' banks and better benefit clubs. He only wishes he had known of a better society before he joined the Black Bear Club.

Pass over another ten years and take another peep at the family. Sons and daughters are married and settled and have families of their own to provide for, and nothing but good wishes for the 'old folks' as they are now called, and who begin to look cheerlessly towards their old age. She is still worth her shilling a day on the farm. He is not worth his 2s 6d. The younger ones would strike for a rise in

**B** Haymaking around 1900

**C** Village life

*their rates of pay if his wages were not reduced, so our old friend has to accept a pay cut of 6d a day. He soon has to make the best of it at 1s 6d. He is as polite and respectable as any man in the parish, and has been blessed with excellent health and spirits. He and the 'old lady' get enough to live on; and so they wear out the time till their health breaks down. A shock of illness comes; it is necessary to nurse him in the workhouse and thus the union opens its doors to receive the old couple, for the wife must go too. They give up the world, sell or give the furniture to their children, and retire to the workhouse for the rest of their lives, doomed to meet no more as man and wife, but once a week for a short half-hour.*

*The old woman is the first to go. She has taken to fretting at being separated from home and husband and in six months dies, of no disease in particular. Then he is left for the first time in his life alone in the world; a feeble old man amongst feeble old men; put into an institution for the first time in his life, and not allowed the small luxuries which have become necessary to him. He dies, and is buried, but his funeral costs nobody much when it comes . . .*  **(A)**

(Reverend J Y Stratton in *The Cornhill Magazine,* February 1864)

## Questions

**1** Look at **A**.
**a** Who or what were the 'bagman clothier' and the 'bagman shoe-maker'?
**b** Why did the farm worker and his wife run into debt early in life?
**c** How did the old couple manage to make ends meet when the husband fell sick?
**d** What do you think a 'sick and benefit club' was?
**e** Who ran the sick and benefit club?
**f** Why was this system open to abuse?
**g** The 'approved system' was a bit like YTS. Can you think why?

**2 a** Describe in detail what you can see in photographs **B** and **C**. Think about: clothing; housing; children; work; friendships.
**b** How reliable are these photographs in providing us with an accur-ate record of country life in the nineteenth century? Would you say the photographs are more reliable than the written extract? Give reasons for your answer.

**3** Use the information in the written sources and the photographs, and your own knowledge of the topic to write the autobiography (a life story written by the person concerned) of a farm worker or his wife in 1864. Try to write about your thoughts, feelings and reactions to the things which happen to you.

# 8 Farming in the 1880s

Flora Thompson was a postmistress from Oxfordshire. In 1939 she wrote a book called *Lark Rise*. In the book she described farm work in the 1880s and 1890s (**A**). **B** and **C** are photographs of farm life from that period.

> *There were usually three or four ploughs to a field, each of them drawn by a team of four horses, with a boy at the head of the leader and the ploughman behind at the shafts. All day, up and down they would go, ribbing the pale stubble with stripes of dark furrows, which, as the day advanced, would get wider and nearer together, until at length, the whole field lay in a rich velvety-plum colour . . .*
>
> *After the plough had done its work, the horse-drawn roller was used to break down the clods; then the harrow to comb out and leave in neat piles the weeds and the twitch grass which infested those fields. Then seed was sown, crops were thinned out and hoed and, in time mown, and the whole process began again.*
>
> *Machinery was just coming into use on the land. Every autumn appeared a pair of large traction engines which, posted one on each side of a field, drew a plough across and across by means of a cable. These toured the district under their own steam for hire on the different farms, and the outfit included a small caravan, known as 'the box', for the two drivers to live and sleep in. In the 'nineties, Laura's brothers did a spell with the steam plough, horrifying the other hamlet people . . .*
>
> *Such machinery as the farmer owned was horse-drawn and only in partial use. In some fields a horse-drawn drill would sow the seeds in rows, in others a human sower would walk up and down with a basket suspended from his neck and fling the seed with both hands broadcast. In harvest time the mechanical reaper was already a familiar sight, but it only did a small part of the work; men were still mowing with scythes and a few women were still reaping with sickles. A threshing machine on hire went from farm to farm and its use was more general; but men at home still threshed their allotment crops with a flail and winnowed the corn by pouring from sieve to sieve in a wind.*

*The labourers worked hard and well when they considered the occasion demanded it and kept up a good steady pace at all times. Some were better workmen than others of course; but the majority took a pride in their craft . . .*

*They were fond of explaining to outsiders that field work was not the fool's job that some townsmen considered it. Things must be done just so and at the exact moment, they said; there were ins and outs in good land work which took a man a lifetime to learn. A few of the lazier men would boast 'We gets ten bob a week, a' we earns every penny of it; but we don't earn no more; we takes hemmed good care of that!' But at team work, at least, such 'Slack-twisted 'uns' had to keep in step, and the pace if slow, was steady.* **(A)**

(Flora Thompson, *Lark Rise*, 1939)

## Questions

**1** According to **A** what were: **a** 'the box'; **b** 'slack-twisted 'uns'; **c** 'broadcast' sowing; **d** winnowing; **e** threshing?

**2 a** Describe the farm tools used by the men in **B**. How do you think a mowing team worked?
**b** How is the threshing-machine in **C** powered? What problems might farmers face when using this source of power?
**c** In what ways do **B** and **C** confirm Flora Thompson's descriptions of farm work in **A**?
**d** What would you say was Flora Thompson's attitude to farm work in the 1880s? Use words or sentences from **A** to support your answer.
**e** Do you think farm workers like those shown in **B** would have been pleased or displeased to see the introduction of machines like **C**? Think carefully before you write your answer!

**3** 'Sources **B** and **C** are more reliable than **A** because they provide a photographic record of farming in the 1880s whereas **A** is just one person's impressions of life on the land.' Do you agree? Give reasons for your answer.

**4** Use all the sources and any other information you can find to write a short essay about British farming techniques in the 1880s. You could mention: ploughing; sowing; reaping; threshing; winnowing; new machinery on farms; the working lives of farm labourers.

**B** Suffolk farmers with scythes

**C** Threshing in Suffolk around 1910

# 9 Women and the 'gang system'

❝An agricultural gang is a number of persons employed by one person, who lets them out to different farmers in turn for certain kinds of work. A gang will number from 12 to 30 persons. The gangs are employed in removing or hoeing up weeds of various kinds, especially twitch, red weed, docks and thistles; stone picking, hoeing turnips, swedes and mangolds, and topping and tailing them. The hours of labour are generally from eight in the morning to five in the afternoon, but the gang may be kept later, as the gangman marks out in the morning a certain amount of land, which must be cleaned or hoed before he dismisses the gang.

The gang will often have to walk three, four, five or even more miles before it starts work, and will have in the evening to return the same distance. The rate of pay is 4d (1½p) to children, 8d (3p) to lads, girls and women. The advantage of the gang to the farmer is that it enables him to sack a certain number of (male) labourers .. he can get help at exactly the time he requires it, and the work is quickly done.

As the gangman asks no questions as to the character of those he employs, the gang will sometimes consist of idle labourers, young women of doubtful character, married women of idle habits and young children ...

The dress of the women is to a certain extent almost indecent. When the crops are wet, they tuck their dresses up between their legs, often leaving the legs much exposed. The long absence and distance from home often make it necessary that the women should attend to the calls of nature, and this they often do in the presence of boys and men.

The conduct of the women and girls belonging to a gang is often offensive in the most public places to passers-by, and their remarks and coarse language distressing and annoying. As mothers they are slatternly, careless about their homes, unconcerned about their children. Girls thus employed can rarely find jobs as domestic servants. To say that a girl has been employed in the fields, in gangs *or otherwise, is usually enough for farmers and tradesmen to reject her application for a job.* **(A)**

(From Mr J E White's report on Agricultural Gangs; Children's Employment Commission, 6th Report, 1867)

❬*I can't speak up for the gangs; they all ought to be done away with . . . Harvest work is different; you are not under a gangmaster . . . and much money can be made; a woman can make 2s 3d (11p) a day, and that comes nice to anyone.*

*A girl whom I took to live, because she has no home to go to, came back today from the gang all dripping wet from the turnips. If you don't feel any hurt from the wet when you are young, you do afterwards, when you are old and the rheumatism comes on . . .*❭ **(B)**

(Rachel Gibson of Castleacre, Norfolk quoted in *Children's Employment Commission*, 6th Report, 1867)

❬*I am convinced that the gang system is the cause of much immorality. The evil in the system is the mixture of the sexes . . . At the infirmary* (hospital) *many girls of 14 years of age, and even girls of 13, have been brought in pregnant to be confined here. The girls have stated that their ruin has taken place in this gang work . . . I have myself seen indecent acts taking place between boys and girls, of 14–16 years of age. I have once seen a young girl assaulted by five or six boys on the road side. Other older persons were 20 or 30 yards off, but they took no notice.*❭ **(C)**

(Dr C Morris quoted in *Children's Employment Commission,* 6th Report, 1867)

❬*Case heard at the Downham Market Session, August 6, 1866.*

*A female child stated: 'I know Collins (the defendant); he is the gangmaster. I remember last Monday week . . . Mr Collins pulled me down and pulled up my clothes, only to my waist. I think there were a dozen in the gang . . . All this was in sight of the gang, we were sitting down to our dinners . . . The other boys and girls in the gang were round me. I called out, the others laughed. He said "Open your legs more." He had a stick. I told my mother after I got home at night . . . Collins hurt my hand when I tried to get up, he was on me, and I could not get up, he was laying on me flat, I was on my back on the ground. I don't know how long he was on me. He* did not say anything to any of the others, but the others saw it. Collins has threatened to flog us, if we told any tales.'

A boy, aged ten, brother of the girl: 'I saw Collins pulling the girls about and showing their backsides. He did it to my sister and two other girls.'

The farmer, employing the gangmaster, an old man of 72, had employed him 30 years. He had always found him an 'honest and upright man' and believed he would act as father to the children. **(D)**

(From Mr J E White's Report, 1867)

It is generally agreed that the employment of women is to a great extent demoralizing . . . Not only does it unsex a woman in dress, gait, manners, character, making her rough, coarse, clumsy, masculine . . . but it makes her unfit for a woman's proper duties at home. **(E)**

(Rev. J Fraser's Report; Employment of Women in Agriculture, 1867)

The increase in women workers was particularly noticeable in the Eastern Counties as a result of the Gang System . . . The system rose to meet the demand for casual labour on large farms.

The gang master had usually been an agricultural labourer himself, and was of the same class as his gang. He benefited by becoming an employer instead of a labourer, and was better off financially. Sometimes he received a small sum for each member of his gang; more often he tried to make a profit by taking piece work from the farmer and paying day wages to the gang. Many of them also made a profit by keeping and selling food and forcing all members of the gang to buy from him.

Morally the results of the gang system were very harmful. The possibility of a job drew young men and women from all districts to the overcrowded open parishes under conditions which led to immoral behaviour.

Although the gang system was condemned in the Report of 1843, it went on and increased for another quarter of a century until public opinion demanded an enquiry which resulted in the regulation of the gangs after 1868. As the Commissioner pointed out in 1843, the evils of the system could not be remedied merely by putting an end to ganging . . . the remedy lay in the hands of the landowners . . . **(F)**

(Ivy Pinchbeck, Women Workers and the Industrial Revolution, 1930)

# Questions

**1 a** What sort of work did the gangs have to do (**A**)?
**b** How many people worked in each gang (**A**)?
**c** How many hours a day did the gangs work (**A**)?
**d** The gang system first appeared in Norfolk. Why did the system become very common in 'Eastern Counties' (**F**)?
**e** According to Rachel Gibson (**B**), what was the difference between gang work and harvest work?

**2 a** Which of the sources, **A–F**, is *not* a primary source?
**b** In what ways do sources **A–F** show bias?
**c** 'Sources **A–F** show bias. Therefore they cannot be regarded as useful historical evidence.' Do you agree?

**3 a** Why did farmers prefer to employ women rather than men?
**b** What attitudes do the authors of **A–E** adopt towards women workers?
**c** Do any of their comments about working women seem unfair?
**d** How have attitudes towards women working outside the home changed over the past 100 years?
**e** How would you feel if your younger brother or sister was treated like the girl in **D**?

**4 a** Sources **A–E** were published in 1867. What effect do you think the reports had on public opinion? If similar reports were published in 1990, do you think public reaction would be any different?
**b** 'The remedy (cure) lay in the hands of the landowners' (**F**). Why did Ivy Pinchbeck think that the landowners could change the gang system?
**c** In 1868 Parliament passed a Gangs Act restricting the gang system. Yet the gang system carried on in a modified form until 1890. Why didn't MPs simply ban the system completely in 1868?

# 10 Women in agriculture

Photographs A–D were taken between 1890 and 1910.

## Questions

**1 a** The following four farming jobs were all done by women during this period. Match them up with pictures **A–D**: **(i)** milking; **(ii)** binding; **(iii)** haymaking; **(iv)** hoeing.

**b** Describe in detail the clothing worn by the women in sources **A–D**. How does their clothing reflect: **(i)** where the women worked; **(ii)** when they worked; **(iii)** the nature of their work; **(iv)** climate?

**c** Would you say these clothes were chosen for comfort or because they were fashionable?

**d** The women all appear to have one piece of outdoor clothing in common. What is it and why was it necessary?

**e** How reliable are these photographs as source material for the historian? You should think about: why the photographs were taken; when and where they were taken; the way people tend to pose or dress up for photographs; technical limitations of early cameras; the advantages and disadvantages of other historical sources.

**f** How and why have these farming jobs changed over the past 80 years? You could mention: an increasing population; World Wars; higher wages; machinery; scientific advances; hygiene; hours of work; trade unions; Acts of Parliament; the decline of the rural population; the women's movement. (See also *Agrarian Britain*, Blackwell History Project.)

**A** Hampshire, 1910

**B** Women at work in Norfolk, 1890

**C** Women farm workers in Northumberland. 1900

**D** A dairy maid in Cardiganshire, Wales, 1897

# 11 The Women's Land Army

While clearing out your attic one day, you find some old documents, pictures and adverts about the Women's Land Army. Someone has cut them out from newspapers, magazines and books during the Second World War. Look through the documents carefully.

❝ *September, 1939. Our immediate task is to bring in the peacetime harvest and get two million extra acres of land ploughed up and under crops by next year. There is not a moment to lose!*

*We intend to set up a number of County War Agricultural Committees. The committees will be composed of practising farmers who will be responsible for directing farm production along the lines of official policy and organising labour in their areas. A WLA Committee will also be appointed for each county.* ❞  (**A**)

❝ *September, 1939. A WLA official told our reporter that there has been no lack of enthusiasm. One girl, asked by telephone on 1st September how soon she could be ready, answered 'Can you give me 20 minutes?'* ❞  (**B**)

❝ *October, 1939. Here was the thing for me – the service to keep England – the service to keep this land alive – and also a service in which one could help in the everlasting process of creation, instead of helping in destruction.* ❞  (**C**)

❝ *July, 1940. Harvesting over, there were many long days scything thistles, picking up apples (cider making was a light relief), picking up four acres of potatoes, hauling roots. My enthusiasm became a little tarnished.* ❞  (**D**)

❝ *For the future, as well as the present, the Land Army must see that not only is the labourer worthy of her hire, but her hire is worthy of the labourer. We had to fight to get our girls a guaranteed*

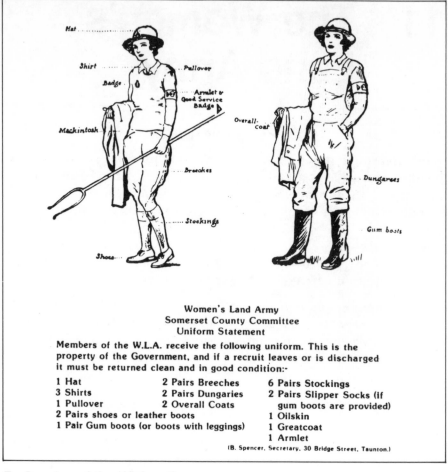

Women's Land Army
Somerset County Committee
Uniform Statement

Members of the W.L.A. receive the following uniform. This is the property of the Government, and if a recruit leaves or is discharged it must be returned clean and in good condition:-

| | | |
|---|---|---|
| 1 Hat | 2 Pairs Breeches | 6 Pairs Stockings |
| 3 Shirts | 2 Pairs Dungaries | 2 Pairs Slipper Socks (if |
| 1 Pullover | 2 Overall Coats | gum boots are provided) |
| 2 Pairs shoes or leather boots | | 1 Oilskin |
| 1 Pair Gum boots (or boots with leggings) | | 1 Greatcoat |
| | | 1 Armlet |

(B. Spencer, Secretary, 30 Bridge Street, Taunton.)

**F**  Drawing of the WLA uniform

*minimum wage of 28 shillings for a 48 hour week; we now have to campaign for 38 shillings for a 45 hour week.* **(E)**

❪ *Although the Land Army was not finally disbanded until 1950, numbers began to fall steadily after the summer of 1944. At the end of the war (1945), many land girls resigned, although a good number stayed to continue the necessary work of food production and 5 000 were to take up permanent jobs on the land.*

*At the close of war, the WLA was not treated with the gratitude it deserved. In February 1945, when the government announced that land girls would not be eligible for resettlement grants offered to Defence workers, Lady Denman (the President of the WLA) resigned in protest. The land girl received no gratuities ('golden handshakes') or civilian clothing allowance. She had to return her uniform, keeping*

"Well, you see, sir, it came out rather thin, so I thought I would run it through again!"

**G** Cartoon satirising new recruits to the WLA

*only one shirt, one pair of shoes and one greatcoat* (overcoat). *She was indeed a Cinderella to the end!* **(H)**

# Questions

**1** Match up the sources listed below with the documents **A–H**.

  **a** A secondary source dealing with the history of the WLA written in October 1984

  **b** A government announcement

  **c** Cartoon from *The Land Girl*

  **d** Interview with Edith Snelgrove 10 months after the outbreak of war

  **e** *Somerset Countryman* (a newspaper)

  **f** Statement by Inez Jenkins, Chief Administrative Officer of the WLA

  **g** Interview with Valerie Hodge, Land Girl No.1

**h** Somerset County Committee Uniform Statement

**2 a** How do the women's working clothes (**F**) differ from the costumes seen in the last chapter (Women in Agriculture: 2)?
**b** What do these differences tell us about changes in attitudes to women during the twentieth century?
**c** In **H**, what does the phrase 'She was a Cinderella to the end' mean?
**d** In what way does **G** show sexism (discrimination against people on the grounds of their sex)? Would you say that the cartoon is poking fun at the farmer, the land girl or both?

# Section II
# INDUSTRY

# 1 The Yorkshire cloth industry

In 1724 Daniel Defoe, a writer and journalist, published *A Tour Through the Whole Island of Great Britain* about his travels in the West Riding of Yorkshire, a centre of the woollen cloth industry. He discovered that the production of woollen cloth had made the area very prosperous (**A**).

> ❪ *This business is the clothing trade . . . such has been the bounty of nature to this otherwise frightful country, that two things essential to the business are found here; I mean coals and running water upon the tops of the highest hills. At every house there was a tenter* (a frame for stretching cloth); *wherever we passed any house we found a little gutter of running water, and at every large house was a manufactory or work-house, and the little streams were so parted and guided by gutters or pipes, and by turning and dividing the streams, that none of those houses were without a river running into and through their workhouses.*
>
> *Then, as every clothier* (cloth-producer) *must keep a horse to fetch and carry for the use of his manufacture, to fetch home his wool and his provisions from market, to carry his yarn to the spinners, his goods to the fulling mill* (where the cloth was shrunk) *and, when finished, to the market to be sold; every manufacturer generally keeps a cow or two, for his family; the manufacturer employs the two, or three, or four pieces of enclosed land about his house, for they scarce sow corn enough for their cocks and hens; and this feeding their grounds still adds by the dung of the cattle, to enrich the soil.*
>
> *Having thus fire and water at every dwelling, there is no need to enquire why they live thus scattered upon the highest hills. Among the wool merchants houses are scattered a large number of cottages in which dwell the workmen who are employed, the women and children of whom are always busy carding and spinning, so that no hands being unemployed, all can gain their bread even from the youngest to the oldest; hardly anyone above four years old, but its hands are sufficient to itself.* ❫ (**A**)

# Questions

**1 a** What is meant by: tenters; clothiers; carding; manufactory; fulling mill?
**b** Which two things 'essential to the (cloth) business' are mentioned in the extract?
**c** Why did people live 'on the highest hills'?
**d** Why was it important for a clothier to own a horse and a manufacturer to own a cow?

**2 a** The system of production described by Defoe is sometimes known as the 'domestic system'. Use the source and your own knowledge of the topic to describe how the domestic system worked.
**b** Use the extract and your own knowledge to explain why the woollen industry of Yorkshire was slower to change over to the factory system than the cotton industry of Lancashire.

# 2 Abraham Darby

The Darby family of Coalbrookdale were some of the most famous iron-producers of the eighteenth century. Abraham Darby I (1677–1717), a Quaker ironmaster, owned a firm in Bristol which made brass and copper cooking-pots. In 1709 he moved his firm to Coalbrookdale in Shropshire where there were plentiful supplies of iron ore, coal and wood. A small tributary of the River Severn, the Cole Brook, had cut a deep valley through coal seams forty feet thick and iron-ore beds twenty-four feet thick. The River Severn provided a navigable waterway from Bristol to Shrewsbury. Samuel Smiles described Darby's early experiments in iron production at Coalbrookdale in his book *The Lives of the Engineers* from which the following extract (**A**) is taken.

❝ *In the year 1709 Darby removed to Coalbrookdale in Shropshire. He took the lease of a little furnace which had existed at the place for more than a century . . . The woods of oak and hazel which filled the beautiful dingles of the dale provided abundant fuel for the smithery. As the trade of the Coalbrookdale firm grew, these woods became cleared, until the same scarcity of fuel began to be experienced that had already desolated the forests of Sussex, and brought the manufacture of iron in that county to a standstill . . .*

*It appears from the 'Blast Furnace Memorandum Book' of Abraham Darby which we have examined that the make of iron at the Coalbrookdale foundry in 1713 varied from five to ten tons a week. The principle articles cast were pots, kettles and other 'hollow ware' direct from the smelting furnace; the rest of the metal was run into pigs. In the course of time we find that other castings were turned out: a few grates, smoothing irons, door frames, weights, baking-plates, cart-bushes, iron pestles, mortars and occasionally a tailor's goose. The trade gradually increased until we find as many as 150 pots and kettles cast in one week. The fuel used in the furnace appears, from the Darby Memorandum Book, to have been at first entirely charcoal; but the growing scarcity of wood seems to have gradually led to the use of coke, brays (small coke) and peat. An abundance of coals existed in the neighbourhood: by rejecting those of an inferior quality and coking the others with great care, a combustible was obtained better fitted even than charcoal itself . . . Thus we find that Darby's most favourite charge for his furnaces was five baskets of coke, two of brays and one of peat; next followed the ore and then the limestone. The use of charcoal was gradually given up as the art of smelting with coke and brays improved, most probably aided by the increased power of the furnace-blast, until at length we find it entirely discontinued.* (A)

# Questions

**1 a** Why did Abraham Darby move the site of his ironworks to Coalbrookdale in 1709?
**b** How did Coalbrookdale get its name?
**c** What sort of iron goods did Darby produce?
**d** What problems did Darby encounter at the new site? How were these solved?

**2** Design a flow-chart to show the link between items in the production of iron: iron ore; wrought iron; pig iron; slag; the blast furnace; charcoal/coke; cast iron; molten iron.

**3 a** Is source **A** a primary or secondary source? Why?
**b** Which primary source did Smiles consult to write his biography of Darby?
**c** Samuel Smiles was a great admirer of Abraham Darby. Why, then, should we treat Smiles' biography of Darby with some caution?

**4 a** What sources of power were used at the ironworks in **B**?
**b** How might the look of the ironworks have changed by 1850?

**B** The ironworks at Coalbrookdale

# 3 The iron king

The Walker family of Rotherham were famous eighteenth-century iron producers. Their iron foundry started off as a small family business in 1741 but by the 1780s had grown into a giant industry (**A**). By the early nineteenth century there were ironworks as far afield as Scotland, South Wales, the West Midlands and Devon (**B**).

❝ *1741*. In or about October 1741, Samuel and Aaron Walker built an air furnace in the old nailor's smithy, on the backside of Samuel Walker's cottage at Grenoside; and after rebuilding the chimney or stacks once, and the furnace once more, began to proceed a little, Samuel Walker teaching the school at Grenoside, and Aaron Walker making nails and mowing and shearing part of his time.

*November, 1743*. This year we made goods to the amount of about ten tons. Aaron Walker now began to be much employ'd, and had four shillings a week to live upon, and the rest of his time or wage balanced what time Samuel Walker could spare from the school.

*November, 1744*. This year we made goods to the amount of $31\frac{1}{2}$ tons. Pulled down the old smithy and huts to the ground, and built a new foundry with two air furnaces and a smithy to it.

*November, 1745*. This year we took about 39 tons of castings; and as we had occasion, took in raw hands such as nailors, husbandmen etc. Samuel Walker, finding business increase, was obliged to give up his school, and built himself a house at the end of the old cottage, then thought he was fixed for life; then we allowed ourselves ten shillings a week each for wages to maintain our families.

*November, 1746*. This year we made $63\frac{1}{2}$ tons of castings; and now a valuation being made of the effects, the capital amounted to £40 000; Jonathan Walker put into stock £10 000; John Crawshaw £5000; Samuel Walker added £5000; which made the capital £60 000.

Samuel Walker began to see the disadvantage of being so far from a navigable river, and with a great deal of trouble decided to start building at Masborough, near Rotherham, where we built a casting house, with two air furnaces and a smithy adjoining . .

*November 1747*. This year we made 96 tons of castings and we supposed the value of the capital then £90 000.

*November, 1748*. This year we made 110 tons of castings, and supposed the value of the capital then £130 000. This year Samuel Walker and Mr Jonathan Booth built the steel furnace at Masborough.

*November, 1749*. This year we made 129 tons of castings, and supposed the value of the capital £180 000. Built a furnace to cast pots in, and a barn adjoining, opposite Aaron Walker's house at Masborough, and a little warehouse adjoining the end of his house; a little counting house and a small place to cast brass in; and a barn at the foundry at Grenoside.

*November, 1758*. This year we made 284 tons of castings and supposed the net stock £8 500. Built a tin house at the forge; corn chambers with cart-houses under, also a hay loft with cart-house under. . . and made a navigable cutt (canal) to near the Eccles; besides very great trouble and expense in opening the ironstone works and colliery and made almost incredible improvements in the road to Holmes from Masborough.

*November, 1763*. This year we made 448 tons of castings and supposed the valuation of the stock to be £15 200. This year the works turned out very well, supposed £3 000 but deducted £1300 for law expenses, losses, interest of money, clerks' wages etc.

*1 May, 1769*. We now suppose the clear value of the company's effects to be £42 500.

*1 May, 1775*. We now suppose the company's effects to be £58 500; tho' there have been great losses by SW and AW.

*1 May, 1777*. We now suppose the company's effects to be £102 000, tho' this may not be thought too high; but when we consider the quantity of guns produced this year, there seems good reason for the above supposition. This year we were bereaved of our partner, A Walker, who died in January after a life of much industry. He had the firm's management of the casting and steel trade in which he showed more ingenuity than patience . . .

*1 May, 1782*. Suppos'd value of capital: £110 000; Add to the above the suppos'd increase since 1 May 1781: £18 000; Divided this 1 May 1782 £28 000; Company's capital £100 000. On the 12 April this firm suffered a terrible loss in the death of the first partner in the firm, Samuel Walker, who has left a widow, four sons and three daughters. Buildings etc., 1782. Thibro' Forge: widen'd the race, put in a new sheel (water wheel) put up a pair of cylinder bellows; put up a new chaffing wheel; built a new counting house at the top of the steps. Built new stables for four horses, coach-house etc. Jordan Dam:

*Pitched 16 or 18 yards in length of the Wear (weir). Rebuilt blast furnaces, storehouses.*
*Holmes: made various alterations to boring and rolling mills. Took the roof off the old blast furnace, raised the walls about six feet, put on a new roof. Erected a new crane. Fire engine completed to blow out three furnaces. This began work in March.* **(A)**

# Questions

**1 a** Look at **A**. Copy and complete the chart below.

| I<br>Year | II<br>Amount of iron produced | III<br>Capital | IV<br>Foundry buildings |
|---|---|---|---|
| 1746 | | | |
| 1747 | | | |
| 1749 | | | |
| 1758 | | | |
| 1763 | | | |
| 1777 | | | |
| 1782 | | | |

**b** Draw a block graph to show the statistics in columns I, II and III.
**c** Look at the company's accounts for 1 May, 1782. Explain how the figure of £100 000 (the company's capital) was arrived at.

**2** According to **A**, how did the Walker brothers improve transport and communications in the Rotherham area?

**3 a** What evidence is there in **A** to suggest that Great Britain was at war in 1777? Which war was it?
**b** What effect do you think this war would have had on the British iron industry?

**3 a** Why was **B** published?
**b** What sort of iron goods were produced in Tavistock?
**c** What did 'the plant' consist of?
**d** What happened to the goods produced at Tavistock ironworks?
**e** Why do you think so much land was attached to the ironworks?

**4 a** Is source **B** less reliable than **A**? Why?
**b** How did the Walker family's ironworks in 1782 differ from the Tavistock ironworks in 1815? How do you explain these differences?
**c** 'The iron industry in the late eighteenth and early nineteenth centuries was in a process of rapid change.' In what ways do sources **A** and **B** confirm or contradict this statement?

## *TAVISTOCK IRON WORKS,*
### TAVISTOCK, DEVON.

# PARTICULARS
#### OF THE
# TAVISTOCK IRON-WORKS,
#### AN EMINENT ESTABLISHED
## *FOUNDERY;*
### *BAR IRON FROM SCRAPS OR BUSHELL IRON;*
### ANCHOR SMITHERY,
#### AND
## *EDGE TOOL MANUFACTORY,*
#### IN AN EXCELLENT SITUATION, NEAR THE
## *TOWN OF TAVISTOCK,*
### In the County of Devon,

Possessing eminent local Advantages, in the Center of an important Mining District, extremely convenient for Trade to PLYMOUTH (distant only 14 Miles), the DOCK, and STONE-HOUSE, also for His Majesty's and Private Yards, Exportation, &c.

## THE PLANT

Comprises Nine powerful Water Wheels, which are plentifully supplied in the dryest Summer, and not liable to be Flooded in Winter; Machinery for Eight Hammers; Air and Blast Furnaces; Four Sets of Blowing Cylinders; a powerful Boring, Rolling, Grinding Mill; and extensive Smithery, and Store-Houses, &c. in a spacious Yard, compact, and inclosed by a Stone-built Wall.

## A RESPECTABLE RESIDENCE,
#### VERY PLEASANTLY SITUATED,
With convenient DOMESTIC OFFICES, STABLE, and a good GARDEN;
#### WITH
*TEN ACRES OF RICH PASTURE LAND, adjoining the Residence:*

## ALSO SEVERAL COTTAGES,

### WITH STABLING, AND REQUISITE OUT-BUILDINGS.

The whole formed at a liberal but judicious Expence, for conveniently and advantageously conducting the Business.

#### *HELD FOR A LONG TERM, AT A LOW GROUND RENT.*

### TO BE SOLD BY AUCTION,
# *BY MR. SCOTT,*
### On *FRIDAY,* the 6th of Oct. 1815, at Twelve o'Clock,
### AT THE MART, LONDON,
#### *Near the Bank of England.*

Unless an acceptable Offer shall be previously made by Private Contract.

#### EARLY POSSESSION MAY BE HAD.
### *The greater Part of the Purchase-Money may remain on Mortgage.*

The Premises may be Viewed by applying to Mr. S. HORNBROOK, at the Manufactory, where descriptive Particulars may be had; also at the Printing Offices of the Cornwall Gazette, Truro; Gazette, Exeter; Telegraph, Plymouth Dock; Cambrian, Swansea; Journal, Bristol; Aris's Gazette, Birmingham; at the Mart; and at the Office of Mr. SCOTT, 28, New Bridge-Street, London, where a Plan of the Premises may be seen.

**B**  Particulars of Tavistock Ironworks, 1815

# 4  Coal mining in the 1830s

Source **A** was published in the 1830s and gives us useful information about coal-mining techniques of 160 years ago.
Study the evidence carefully and answer the questions below.

## Questions

**1** List the three dangers facing coal miners in the 1830s described in **A**.

**2** How can you tell that steam-power was used to lift men and coal up and down shafts **X** and **W**?

**3 a** Where did a pit disaster occur 'some time ago' and how many people were killed in the disaster?
**b** Can you think of a reason why this disaster may have occurred?

**4** What were: spurns; sprogs; hurriers; banksmen; the sump; hangers-on?

**5** What was the importance of the safety lamp (**Z**) in coal mining?

**6** What does the poem tell us about the life of a coal miner in the 1830s?

**7 a** The print forms part of a nineteenth century broadsheet. Thousands of these were sold to the general public in the 1830s. They cost a few pence each. Can you think of three reasons why these prints were so popular in the eighteenth and nineteenth centuries?
**b** Why would such a broadsheet sell comparatively few copies today?

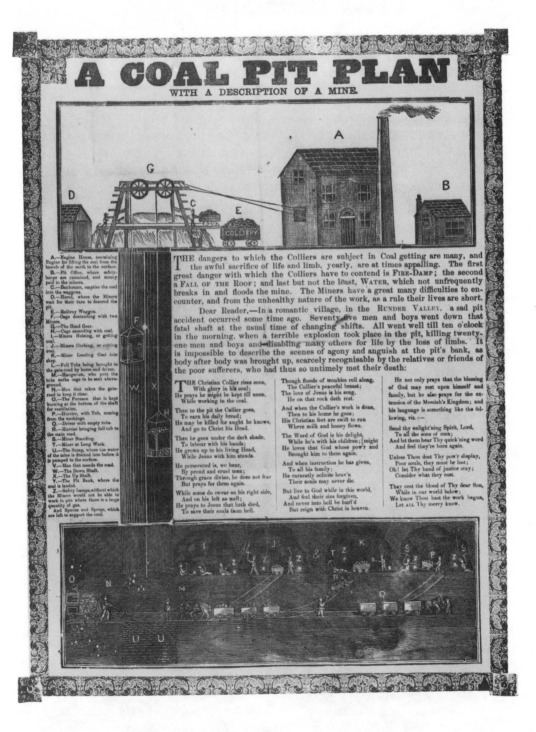

**A** Plan of a coal pit in 1830

# 5 The steam engine

The steam engine shown in **A** is one of the most important inventions of the eighteenth century. The picture shows one of the first engines to be built by Thomas Newcomen (1663–1729), a Devon blacksmith and ironmonger. It was constructed at Dudley Castle in the West Midlands in 1712. The print is dated 1719.

Source **B** is a photograph of a James Watt steam engine built in 1788. It is the oldest steam engine in existence to embody all James Watt's inventions. It was used at Matthew Boulton's Soho Ironworks for 70 years driving 43 metal polishing machines. You can still see this steam engine in the Science Museum, London.

**B** A James Watt steam engine built in 1788

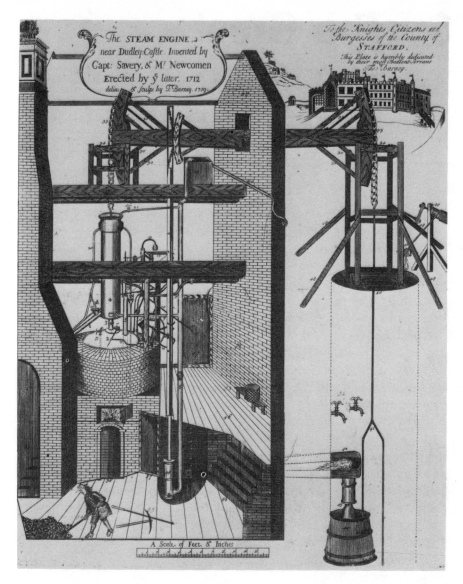

**A** Thomas Newcomen's steam engine

# Questions

**1** Explain in your own words how a steam engine like **A** works. (You should refer to other textbooks if necessary.)

**2 a** You have been asked to give a talk on the history of the steam engine. You are allowed to use one picture to illustrate part of your talk. Would you use **A** or **B**? Give reasons for your choice.

**b** To what uses was steam power put in the nineteenth century? Why was 'The Age of Steam' almost a thing of the past by the early twentieth century?

# 6 The Great Exhibition of 1851

❟ *At first the idea of an Exhibition was far from popular. In some quarters Prince Albert's interest was enough to make people oppose it. Victoria's German husband did not go down well with the 'huntin', shootin' and fishin'' port-drinking aristocrats of England, who were bored by his interest in the arts and his schemes for workmen's houses and designs in industry. The only person who believed in him was the serious young Queen who longed for her people to love and respect him as she did.* ❟ **(A)**

(John Langdon Davies (ed.), *The Great Exhibition, 1851*, 1971)

❟ *Colonel Charles de Laet Waldo Sibthorp was the right-wing, ultra-protestant Tory MP for Lincoln. A man of strange dress and manner, he had successfully opposed the granting of £50 000 a year to Prince Albert because he, the Colonel, did not like foreigners. He was against granting religious freedom to Catholics through his dislike of Catholicism. He had always opposed Railway Bills because he, personally, opposed railways. He was against parliamentary reform and free trade. Early in 1850, he had fought the Public Libraries Act because he did not care for reading. As an enemy of free trade he opposed the idea of an international exhibition but it was not until the matter of the trees came before the Commons that he gained much support.* ❟ **(B)**

(Patrick Beaver, *The Crystal Palace*, 1970)

❟ *It is the greatest trash, the greatest fraud, and the greatest imposition ever to be palmed upon the people of this country. The object of its organisers is to introduce among us foreign stuff of every description – live and dead stock – without regard to quantity or quality. It is meant to bring down prices in this country and to pave the way for setting up the cheap and nasty trash and trumpery system . . . It would be better for the organisers to encourage British industry and support the industrious people of Britain. All the bad characters at present scattered over the country will be attracted to*

*Hyde Park. That being the case, I would advise persons living near the park to keep a sharp lookout after their silver forks and spoons and servant maids.*

*Are the elms in Hyde Park to be cut down to make way for one of the greatest frauds and absurdities ever known? Are they really going to spend £26 000 on this building when the Irish poor are starving? 'Live and let live!' is my motto!*❜ **(C)**

(From a speech by Colonel Sibthorp to the House of Commons, June 18, 1850)

❛*We are to have a huge building of brick, and iron and stone, calculated to endure the wear and tear of the next hundred years. In fact, a building is to be put up in Hyde Park as big as Buckingham Palace. Not only is the vast pile of masonry to be heaped up in the park but one feature of the plan is that there shall be a dome of 200 feet in diameter – larger than the dome of St Paul's . . .*

*The whole of Hyde Park and the whole of Kensington Gardens will be turned into a camp for all the vagabonds of London. By the stroke of a pen our pleasant park – nearly the only spot where Londoners can get a breath of fresh air – will be turned into something between Wolverhampton and Greenwich Fair. The erection of a huge building on such a site will lead to the destruction of the park. We feel the exhibition site should be moved to Regent's Park or Battersea . . .*

*The project looks so like insanity that we can hardly bring ourselves to believe that the advisers of the Prince had dared to connect his name with such an outrage. Can anyone be weak enough to suppose that a building erected on this scale will ever be removed? It will certainly remain a fixture. The first and main reason, therefore, why we protest against the erection of this huge building on such a site is that it means the mutilation of Hyde Park. Once more we beg the Prince and his advisers to think again before it is too late.*❜ **(D)**

(*The Times*, 25 June 1850)

❛*Further to distress us, the whole public, led on by 'The Times' has all at once made a set against me and the Exhibition on the ground of interference with Hyde Park. We are to pack out of London with our nuisance to somewhere like the Isle of Dogs. There is to be a vote in the House of Commons about it today. Peel was to have taken the lead in our defence but since his tragic death on 2 July, there is no-one with influence enough to get a hearing for justice and reason. If we are beaten, we shall have to give the whole thing up.*❜ **(F)**

(Letter from Prince Albert to the Duke of York, 4 July 1850)

**E** Brunel's design for the exhibition building, 1850

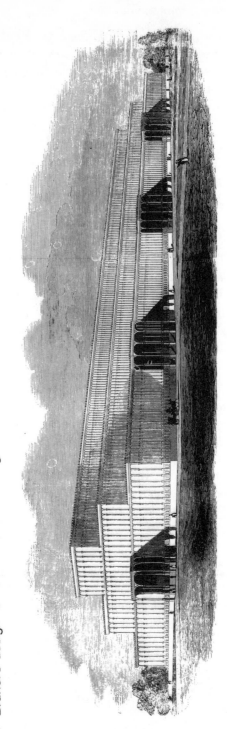

**H** Paxton's original design for the Great Exhibition

❝ With less than 22 weeks to go before the Exhibition building must be ready to receive exhibits, news leaked out that Mr Joseph Paxton has submitted a revolutionary new design. The Committee makes no public comment, but the 'Illustrated London News' publishes a drawing. The magazine supports its adoption for it has been planned with a view to its fitness for the objects intended, as well as for its removal to another site for a winter garden. Built of glass and iron, the building is expected to 'form a peculiar novelty in mechanical science' as well as looking very much more attractive than the official design. ❞  (G)

(Illustrated London News, 6 July 1850)

❝ Mathematicians have worked out that the Crystal Palace will blow down in the first strong gale. Engineers have said that the galleries will crash in and destroy the visitors. Economists have predicted a shortage of food in London owing to the vast numbers of people. Doctors say that owing to so many races coming together, the Black Death of the Middle Ages will reappear as it did after the Crusades. Moralists believe that England will be affected by all the unpleasant diseases of the civilised and uncivilised world. Religious maniacs preach that this second Tower of Babel will draw upon it the vengeance of God.

Well, I can give no guarantee against these perils, nor can I be responsible for the lives of your Royal relatives . . . ❞  (J)

(Letter from Prince Albert to the King of Prussia, March 4, 1851)

❝ There were 7 381 exhibitors from the British Isles and 6 556 from other countries. The machinery and manufacturing sections were dominated by Britain. Railway locomotives, boats, bridges, textiles and machine tools showed the progress of steam power and the supremacy of iron. Other manufactures included telescopes, cameras, barometers, an electric telegraph and surgical instruments . . .

'God bless my dear country which has shown itself so great today' wrote Queen Victoria in her diary on May 1 1851, the day of the opening of the Exhibition. In the next five and a half months, before it closed on 11 October, over six million visitors came to the Crystal Palace . . . In the end, a clear profit of £186 437 was made . . . The money was well used. An 87-acre site was purchased in South Kensington, where today the Victoria and Albert Museum, the Science Museum, The Royal College of Art and Music, the Royal Albert Hall and many other fine buildings stand. ❞  (K)

(R J Cootes, Britain Since 1700, 1968)

**L** The Crystal Palace

# Questions

**1 a** List the reasons why Colonel Sibthorp and *The Times* opposed the idea of holding a 'Great Exhibition'.
**b** Would you say any of these criticisms were justified?
**c** Some historians have suggested that Sibthorp was a crank. If this is true, why do you think so many people listened to him in 1850?

**2 a** How did Brunel's design for the exhibition building (**E**) differ from Paxton's first design (**H**)?
**b** How and why was Paxton's design modified between 1850 and 1851?
**c** Why was Paxton's design considered to be 'revolutionary' (**G**)?

**3 a** Why was Albert so unpopular with certain members of the ruling class?
**b** What were Albert's main worries about the exhibition?
**c** How did Albert react to criticism of the proposed exhibition?

**4** Look at **K**.
**a** Calculate the total number of exhibitors at the exhibition.
**b** What percentage of the total number of exhibitors were British?
**c** What was the average daily, weekly and monthly attendance at the exhibition? (The exact number of visitors was 6 039 195.)

**5 a** What opposition, if any, might there be to the idea of holding a Great Exhibition today?
**b** Exhibitions were held in 1851 and 1951 in London. If an exhibition is held in 2051, how do you think it will differ from the previous two?

# 7 The Bessemer Converter

❝Henry Bessemer (1813–1898) was an amazing inventor. He produced a machine for putting perforations on postage stamps, a method of making gold powder, a sugar press, a way of making imitation velvet and a new method of making plate glass.

During the Crimean War (1854–1856), he became interested in the production of iron and steel. The government asked Bessemer to produce a new type of cannon which would not shatter under the force of a shell being fired from it. Bessemer decided to make a gun which combined the best qualities of wrought iron and cast iron – a gun made of steel. Steel-making was a slow and expensive process and so Bessemer started work on a cheap, reliable way of making steel. In 1856 he came up with the idea of the converter.

The converter was a long, pear-shaped vessel which looked like a huge cement-mixer. Molten pig iron was poured into the converter and a blast of hot air was blown through its base. The blast drove out impurities in the molten iron which were turned into burning gases or slag. In about 20 minutes the iron was pure and small amounts of carbon and manganese were added to it to produce mild steel. This type of steel is neither as brittle nor as hard as cast steel. It is ideal for making girders, rails, tools or wire ropes.❞  **(A)**

(S Mason, Work Out Social and Economic History, 1988)

❝Though the essential principle of the invention – the burning out of the carbon in the pig iron – was sound, and has remained the basis of the 'Bessemer' steelmaking to the present day, the converter could not, in fact, produce a commercially usable metal. It required the work of a metallurgist, Robert Mushet (1811–1891) to point out the need for the addition of a small quantity of manganese to the molten metal in the converter. Even with Mushet's modification, the Bessemer converter would only work well with non-phosphoric pig iron; and since the great majority of the British iron ores were phosphoric, this was a serious limitation. It was not until 22 years later that Gilchrist-Thomas solved the problem of the conversion of phosphoric pig iron.❞  **(B)**

(M W Flinn, Readings in Economic and Social History, 1964)

❛I well remember how anxiously I awaited the blowing of the first seven cwt (hundred weight) of pig iron. I had employed an ironmaster's foreman to manage the converter and the melting of the iron. When his metal was nearly all melted, he came to me and said 'Where be going to put the metal, maister?' I said 'I want you to run it by a gutter into that little furnace from which you have just raked out all the fuel, and then I shall blow cold air through it to make it hot.' The foreman replied 'But it will soon be all of a lump.' The metal was run in, and I awaited the result with much impatience . . . After an interval of ten minutes, a huge white flame appeared which rushed out of the space in the upper chamber and brilliantly lit up the whole space around. I watched with some anxiety for the flame to die down as the carbon burnt out. It took place very suddenly. The furnace was then tapped, and out rushed a stream of liquid iron, almost too bright for the eye to rest upon . . . It was allowed to flow vertically into the mould. After eight minutes the ingot (oblong metal bar) rose out of the mould and stood there ready for removal . . . It is impossible for me to convey any idea of my feelings when I saw the metal rise from the mould. In one compact block we had as much metal as could be made by two puddlers and two assistants working for hours with much wastage of fuel. We had obtained a pure ten-inch ingot as a result of thirty minutes blowing, with no skilled labour or fuel. The outcome of the puddlers' labour would have been ten or a dozen impure, shapeless puddle-balls.

I gazed with delight on the first of many thousands of ingots that now come into existence every day. At the date I am writing (1897), the world's present production of Bessemer steel, if cast into ingots ten inches wide and thirty inches in length, weighing 7 cwt each, would make over 90 000 such ingots in every working day of the year . . .

I desired to obtain the unbiased view of some famous engineer who might take a different view of my invention . . . I knew Mr George Rennie very well by reputation, and I invited him to a private view of my process . . . He said 'This is such an important invention that you ought not to keep it secret for another day.' I said 'It is not yet quite a commercial success, and I think I had better perfect it before allowing it to be seen.' 'Oh,' he said, 'All the little details will come naturally to the ironmaster; your great principle is an unqualified success: no fuel, little labour, no puddle-balls, no welding; huge masses of any shape made in a few minutes.'❜  (C)

(Sir Henry Bessemer, *An Autobiography*, 1905)

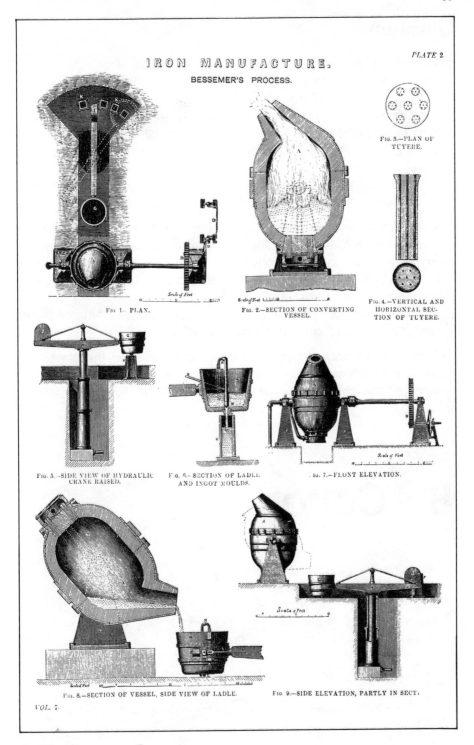

IRON MANUFACTURE.

BESSEMER'S PROCESS.

PLATE 2.

FIG. 3.—PLAN OF TUYERE.

FIG. 1.—PLAN.

FIG. 2.—SECTION OF CONVERTING VESSEL.

FIG. 4.—VERTICAL AND HORIZONTAL SECTION OF TUYERE.

FIG. 5.—SIDE VIEW OF HYDRAULIC CRANE RAISED.

FIG. 6.—SECTION OF LADLE AND INGOT MOULDS.

FIG. 7.—FRONT ELEVATION.

FIG. 8.—SECTION OF VESSEL, SIDE VIEW OF LADLE.

FIG. 9.—SIDE ELEVATION, PARTLY IN SECT.

VOL. 7.

**D** The Bessemer Converter

# Questions

**1** Answer the following questions using *all* the sources.
  **a** Why did Bessemer become interested in metallurgy?
  **b** Describe in detail how the converter worked.
  **c** Why was the converter an improvement on previous methods of making iron and steel?
  **d** What were the drawbacks of using a Bessemer converter to make steel?
  **e** How did the introduction of the converter affect iron and steel production in the second half of the nineteenth century?

**2 a** Source **C** is taken from Bessemer's autobiography. What is an autobiography? Why do historians have to be wary of the evidence contained in an autobiography?
  **b** How does **C** show bias? You should quote words and/or sentences from the source in your answer.
  **c** What evidence is there in **C** to suggest that Bessemer was not sure how well the converter would work?

**3** If you had to write a history of the steel industry in the nineteenth century, what other sources and statistics would you want to look at? How could you check that information contained in these sources was accurate?

# 8  Cotton

---

❝ In the first place we've got the only climate in the world where cotton goods in any quantity can ever be made. In the second, no foreign johnnies can ever be bred that can spin and weave like Lancashire lads and lasses. In the third place there are more spindles in Oldham than in the rest of the world put together. And last of all, if they had the climate, the men and the spindles, which they never can have, foreigners would never find the brains Lancashire men have for the job. ❞  (A)

(William Harrison, a Lancashire cotton manufacturer, quoted in 1911)

**B** Young boy using a spinning mule, Manchester, 1909

|            | 1787 | 1835  | 1870  |
|------------|------|-------|-------|
| Cheshire   | 8    | 109   | 138   |
| Derbyshire | 22   | 93    | 104   |
| Lancashire | 41   | 683   | 780   |
| Yorkshire  | 11   | 126   | 145   |
| England    | 119  | 1 071 | 1 821 |
| Wales      | 4    | 5     | 11    |
| Scotland   | 19   | 159   | 172   |

**C** Cotton factories 1787–1870

68

*The high standard of the textile machinery by which Britain won her industrial leadership has enabled it to be worked fairly well by backward races. Britain is at a steadily increasing disadvantage in trading, not just with people like the Japanese, but also in places where there are plentiful supplies of cheap labour. Of course, the Englishman can borrow money more quickly and cheaply than anyone else. But England's place among the nations in the future depends on the extent to which she retains industrial leadership. Many of the sons of factory owners are content to follow mechanically the lead given by their fathers. They work shorter hours and exert themselves less to obtain practical ideas than their fathers had done; thus a part of England's leadership was rapidly destroyed.* **(D)**

(Alfred Marshall, Official Papers, 1926)

| Year | 1771 | 1801 | 1831 | 1861 | 1891 | 1921 | 1951 |
|---|---|---|---|---|---|---|---|
| Pop. (millions) | 7.5 | 8.9 | 13.9 | 20.1 | 29 | 37.9 | 43.8 |

**E** The Population of Great Britain, 1771–1951

| Year | 1771 | 1801 | 1831 | 1861 | 1891 | 1921 | 1951 |
|---|---|---|---|---|---|---|---|
| Imports | 2.5 | 56 | 263 | 1257 | 1995 | 1204 | 928 |
| Re-exports | 0.29 | 4.4 | 219 | 298 | 1618 | 157 | 75.2 |

**F** Raw Cotton Imports and Re-exports, 1781–1931 (in millions of lbs.)
(Statistics for **C** and **E** from *Abstract of British Historical Statistics*, B R Mitchell and P Deane, 1962)

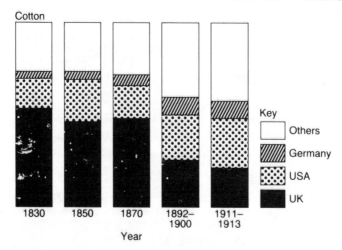

**G** World industry in the nineteenth century (Statistics from *Industry and Empire*, E J Hobsbawm 1968)

❛Whoever says Industrial Revolution says cotton. When we think of it we see the new and revolutionary city of Manchester whose population multiplied ten times between 1760 and 1830 ... The British Industrial Revolution was by no means only cotton, or Lancashire or even textiles, and cotton lost its importance after 60 years. Yet cotton was the pacemaker of industrial change ...

The manufacture of cotton was a by-product of the increasing current of trade with the British colonies. Its raw material, first used in Europe to produce fustian (linen and cotton), came from the colonies. The English woollen industry succeeded in 1700 in banning the import of cotton goods from India, thus accidentally succeeding in giving domestic cotton producers a free run of the home market ... Until 1770 over 90% of British cotton exports went to the colonies, mainly to Africa. The great expansion of exports after 1750 gave the industry its impetus; between then and 1770, cotton exports multiplied ten times over.

The British cotton industry was certainly in its time the best in the world but it ended, as it began, by relying on contact with the colonies and Third World. Its days were numbered after the First World War when the Indians, Chinese and Japanese made or even exported their own cotton goods and could no longer be prevented from doing so by British interference.❜  **(H)**

(E J Hobsbawm, *Industry and Empire*, 1968)


❛More raw cotton became available as the Southern States of the USA expanded their cotton fields using slave labour, and this supply increased greatly when Eli Whitney, in 1793, developed a cotton gin which speeded up the cleaning of the raw cotton. The spinning section of the work was extremely slow and used a lot of domestic labour; but a series of inventions revolutionised the whole spinning industry. Although the inventions could be used for most of the textile industry, they were first taken up in the cotton industry. Perhaps this was because it was a relatively new industry and so had easier opportunities for growth; but the most likely explanation is the simplest – once the problem of the supply of raw cotton and the problem of the speed of spinning and weaving in quantity had been overcome, there were better entrepreneurs (businessmen) in the cotton industry, capable of realising cotton's potential.❜  **(J)**

(R B Jones, *Economic and Social History of England 1770–1977*, 1979)

# Questions

**1 a** What evidence is there in sources **A** to **J** to suggest that cotton production increased 1770–1870?
**b** According to the sources, why did the demand for cotton increase?

**2 a** Which pieces of evidence **A** to **J** are not primary sources?
**b** Which sources refer to machines like those shown in **B**?
**c** In what way do the statistics in **C** support the text in **H**?

**3** Using all available statistics in this chapter answer the following questions.
**a** What was the population of Great Britain in 1801?
**b** What was the increase in cotton imports 1801–1921?
**c** What proportion of the world's cotton was produced in Britain in 1830?
**d** Which county was the third largest cotton-producing area in 1870?

# 10   Fosdyke's mill

The map on the opposite page shows part of Lancashire in 1770. John Fosdyke, a wealthy cotton merchant has decided to build a cotton mill in or close to the market town of Accersley (population 1 000). Fosdyke looks at three possible sites: **A**, **B** and **C**. Which one should he choose? (Note that the River Ribble is navigable up to point **A**.) You should think about: communications; water supply; coal supply; the labour force; raw materials.

**1** In groups discuss the advantages and disadvantages of each site. Then write a short report on your findings. Mark in the position of the mill.

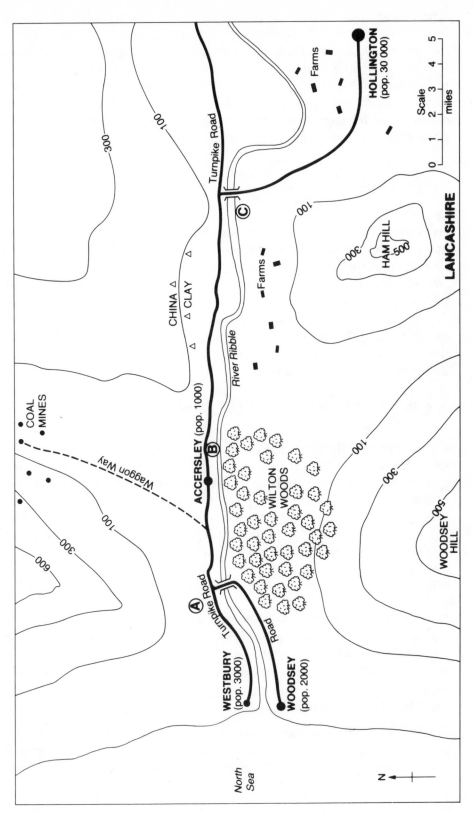

HOLLINGTON
(pop. 30 000)

Farms

Turnpike Road

300

100

Scale
0 1 2 3 4 5
miles

CHINA △
△ CLAY
△

△

C

Farms

100

River Ribble

HAM HILL
300
500

LANCASHIRE

COAL
MINES

Waggon Way

ACCERSLEY (pop. 1000)

B

WILTON
WOODS

100

300

100

300

600

WOODSEY
HILL
500

A

Turnpike Road

Road

WESTBURY
(pop. 3000)

WOODSEY
(pop. 2000)

North
Sea

N

Thirty years pass. The mill is making large profits. John Fosdyke's son, William, takes over the running of the factory. A local canal company decides to build a canal from Hollington to Woodsey. Fosdyke is willing to provide funds for the canal as the turnpike road is in poor condition. However, he wants the canal to run within two miles of his factory. Which route should the canal follow? You should consider: water supply; advantages and disadvantages of canal transport; seepage; locks and aqueducts; access to the canal.

2 In your groups, discuss the possible routes the canal could follow. On your maps mark in the route the group thinks is best.

Forty years later, a railway company builds a line from Liverpool, 20 miles south of Woodsey, to Hollington. There are plans to extend the railway northwards. John Fosdyke's grandson provides the railway company with £10 000 and land near his factory on condition that the line runs within two miles of his cotton mill. The company agrees and the line is built. Considerations are: the canal company's opposition to railways; the cost of cuttings, embankments, bridges; the advantages of railways over other forms of transport; the problems associated with early railways.

3 Mark the best possible route of the railway on your map.

Cotton famine! Between 1861 and 1865 a civil war in America halts the supply of cotton reaching Lancashire. The Fosdykes are not getting enough raw cotton to provide their employees with work. Profits start to fall. Soon the family is in debt. What should they do? The options are: close the factory down temporarily; lay off workers; sell the factory and the land around it; attempt to manufacture other textiles; attempt to import raw cotton from India and China.

4 In your groups decide which option(s) to adopt.

By 1920 the Fosdyke's family business is barely breaking even. The cotton industry has not recovered from the cotton famine of the 1860s and the economic slumps of the 1860s and 1870s. The canal ceased to carry traffic in 1900 although the roads in the area have been improved. In 1925 the firm goes bankrupt and the business is sold off. The mill becomes derelict.

Fifty years later, however, a new motorway is to be built, running north to south between Hollington and Accersley. Which route will the motorway follow? Bear in mind the motorway needs to be level and straight; the motorway will need bridges, service-stations and access roads; the motorway will run north to south and cross the River Ribble at some point between Hollington and Accersley.

5 Mark in the route of the motorway on your map.

In 1990 the derelict mill and the land surrounding it are purchased by Stephen Williamson, a wealthy descendant of John Fosdyke. He decides to set up a new business in the mill. The population distribution of Westbury, Woodsey and Accersley is shown below.

| Age | Under 15 | 16–24 | 25–44 | 45–60 | 61+ |
|---|---|---|---|---|---|
| Westbury | 5 000 | 7 000 | 6 000 | 4 000 | 8 000 |
| Woodsey | 8 000 | 6 000 | 4 000 | 7 000 | 6 000 |
| Hollington | 12 000 | 15 000 | 11 000 | 3 000 | 2 000 |

What sort of business should Williamson set up in Fosdyke's Mill? His options are: an industrial museum; a rural craft centre; sheltered housing; a high technology centre; a health farm.

6 Williamson has £2 million to spend. What would you advise him to do?

# 11 Industrial change

Historians have been discussing the effects of the Industrial Revolution on people's working lives for nearly 200 years. More recently, historians have been arguing about changes in the standard of living. Did living standards rise or fall between 1780 and 1830 or between

1800 and 1850? Did *real wages* (the amount of goods money can buy) rise or fall during these periods? Were people more contented before or after the Industrial Revolution?

These arguments still go on today. As fresh evidence comes to light, people's views and ideas change. Read the extracts below carefully. Would you describe yourself as a 'pessimist' or an 'optimist' (see **D**)?

> ❝ *There were trim villages, with a neat or handsome parsonage and grey church in the midst; there was the pleasant tinkle of the blacksmith's anvil, the patient cart-horse waiting at his door; the basket-maker peeling his willow wands in the sunshine; the wheelwright putting the last touch to a blue cart with red wheels; at the well, clean and comely women carrying yoked buckets, and towards the free school small Britons dawdling on, handling the marbles in the pockets of unpatched corduroys adorned with brass buttons. The land around was rich and marly, great corn-stacks stood in the rickyards; the homesteads were those of rich farmers who paid no rent. The passenger on the coach could see that old England was the best of all possible countries: a nation of clean little market towns without factories, of fat livings, an upper-class clergy and low poor rates.* ❞  (**A**)

(George Eliot, *Felix Holt the Radical*, 1867)

> ❝ *An historian has written of 'the disasters of the industrial revolution'. If he means that technical and economic changes were the source of disaster, the opinion is surely wrong . . . If England had remained a nation of farmers and craftsmen, there would surely have been widespread famine and disease. There are today on the plains of India and China men and women, plague-ridden and hungry, living lives little better than those of the cattle that toil with them by day and share their places of sleep by night. Such standards, and such horrors are the lot of those who increase their numbers without passing through an industrial revolution.* ❞  (**B**)

(T S Ashton, *The Industrial Revolution*, 1948)

> ❝ *The Industrial Revolution destroyed the Domestic System and there is no evidence that in doing so it made life better for the people. If anything, it did the opposite. A valuable way of life in which people respected one another was destroyed. There is no dispute about the fact that the poor grew poorer, simply because the country, and its rich and middle class, so obviously grew richer. The very moment when the poor were at the end of their tether – in the early and middle forties – was the moment when the middle class had plenty of money to invest in wild railway schemes . . .* ❞  (**C**)

(E J Hobsbawm, *Industry and Empire*, 1968)

**F** 'Life for workers in pre-industrial Britain could be very harsh indeed'

❝ *Both Dr Hobsbawm (a 'pessimist') and Professor Ashton (an 'optimist') agree that real wages went down during the wars with France and immediately afterwards. Dr Hobsbawm will not accept that there was any improvement in the standard of living until the mid-1840s. Professor Ashton, on the other hand, believed there was a better economic climate after 1821. In fact the standard of living for most people was bad in 1790; it remained bad in 1830. There were increases in real wages among organized workers during the period of good trade between 1832 and 1834; but the period of good trade between 1833 and 1837 was accompanied by the smashing of the trade unions by the government and employers; while 1837–1842 are depression years. So that it is between 1837 and 1851 that the tide begins to turn. In half a century of industrialism, the standard of living still remained for very large groups – at the point of subsistency* (earning just enough money to live on). ❞  **(D)**

(E P Thompson, *The Making of the Working Class*, 1963)

**G**  Life in a London slum, 1872

❛ *Because of the ugly, dirty, smoky world that resulted from industrial change, many writers began to look back to a time when they imagined people lived pleasant lives in pretty villages taking a craftsman's pride in their work. When we read of the sufferings of nineteenth century workers in their towns, it is easy to fall into the same error ourselves. The reality of life for workers in pre-industrial Britain could be very harsh indeed, even when many were able to gain some money and food from part-time farming and so to some degree were cushioned against times of bad trade.* ❜  **(E)**

(R B Jones, *Economic and Social History of England*, 1971)

# Questions

**1** Explain what is meant by: real wages; subsistency; standard of living; Industrial Revolution.

**2 a** In what ways do **F** and **G** confirm or contradict the evidence in the written sources?

**b** Does R B Jones (**E**) support Ashton's view of the Industrial Revolution (**B**) or Hobsbawm's view (**D**)?

**c** Dr Hobsbawm and Professor Ashton are both famous historians. Many students admire their work. Why do you think they disagree so markedly over the effects of the Industrial Revolution?

**3** In what ways do sources **A** to **G** show bias? In your answer you could mention: who wrote, drew or took them; when they were written or made; what the writers or artists thought of agrarian Britain, the Industrial Revolution and changes in the standard of living.

**4** Tell the story of someone who began their working life in some form of cottage industry in 1800 and ended their working life in a factory in 1850. In your writing you could mention: working conditions; wages; changes in the appearance of the countryside; living conditions; food; the discipline of factory life; Factory Acts.

# Section III
# TRANSPORT

# 1 Stand and deliver!

Who was the real Dick Turpin?

> ❝It is 1739. The shadows reveal a well-dressed gentleman in his early twenties. He speaks in an educated accent. 'Everyone has heard of me. My name is Dick Turpin. I come from a good family and had an expensive education. I was so bored leading the life of a well-bred gentleman that I took to highway robbery as a form of amusement. I robbed only the rich and any profits from my activities were given to the poor. I rode my horse "Black Bess" to York on one occasion in order to establish an alibi.❞  **(1)**

> ❝A scruffy individual appears. 'I ain't much to say. I'm the real Turpin. I'm just your ordinary sort of highway robber. I steal because I need the money. It's as simple as that. Yes. I've caved in a few skulls in my time but only if I was set on first. My father worked in a slaughterhouse and my mother was a washerwoman. I got done by the law for cattle-stealing in 1739.❞  **(2)**

> ❝I was born in Essex, a butcher's son. I followed my father's trade and 'borrowed' a few dead cattle from a mate in Waltham Abbey so that I could keep the business running. I got involved in poaching and a bit of housebreaking before taking to the road as a highwayman. I once killed a man in self-defence and accidentally shot one of my best mates, Tom King. In 1739 I was arrested and charged with horse-stealing. I now await my fate.❞  **(3)**

You have almost certainly heard of Dick Turpin, the famous highwayman. Which description (**1**, **2** or **3**) would you say gives the most accurate picture of Turpin? Now read through these original sources.

> ❝We hear that for the past six weeks, Blackheath has been so plagued by highwaymen (supposed to be Rowden and Turpin), that 'tis dangerous for travellers to pass. On Thursday, Turpin and Rowden had the cheek to ride through the City at noon, and in Watling Street

*were known to two or three porters, who had not the courage to attack them. They went towards the bridge; so 'tis thought they are gone on the Tonbridge Road.* **(A)**

(*Grub Street Journal*, October 16 1735)

*Your friend, Mr Colling, was surprised last year near Cambridge by the famous Turpin. The highwayman, after having repeated in vain the command to stand, fired at him. Although the shot missed him, Mr Colling decided to obey. The highwayman took his money, his watch and his snuff-box, leaving him only two shillings to continue his journey.* **(B)**

(J B Le Blanc, *Letters on the English and French Nations*, 1737)

*A reward of £100 had been offered for Turpin's capture. Thomas Morris, one of the keepers of Epping Forest, accompanied by a pedlar, set off to catch him. Turpin saw them approaching his dwelling. He noticed that Morris was carrying a gun and thought he was a poacher. On which he said 'You'll find no hares in this part of the forest.' 'No,' said Morris, 'but I have found a Turpin.' Raising his gun, he told Turpin to surrender. Turpin spoke to him in a friendly manner and gradually retreated at the same time, till, having seized his own gun, he shot him dead. The pedlar ran off quickly.*

*This proclamation has been issued by the government: 'It has been made known to the King that Richard Turpin did cruelly murder Thomas Morris, one of the keepers of Epping Forest and is pleased to promise a reward of £200 for any persons that can catch him so that he can be tried and convicted. Turpin was born at Thaxted in Essex, is about 30, by trade a butcher, about five feet nine inches tall, very much marked with the smallpox, his cheekbones broad, his face thinner towards the bottom, his visage short, pretty upright and broad about the shoulders.* **(C)**

(From *The Newgate Calendar*, May 1737)

Turpin gave this account to the hangman at the gallows in May 1739.

*I was bred a butcher and served for five years at Whitechapel. Falling into idle company, I went into highway robbery and gained some small reward from this. There was no attempt made to capture me and I began to commit robberies in Epping Forest. One day, having obtained no booty, I met with Mr Thompson's servant. I had turned my horse loose and asked of Mr Thompson's man if he had seen a horse. Then Mr Thompson's servant answered 'I know nothing of Turpin's horse, but I have found Turpin!' He then aimed his blunderbuss at me but I jumped behind a broad oak. I fired my carbine at Thompson's servant and shot him dead.*

*I later fell into partnership with Tom King, who was hanged in London some time ago. Once, we were nearly captured and I fired a pistol into the hostile crowd. By mistake I shot Tom in the leg. I confess I am guilty of many crimes but there are also robberies I have been charged with which I did not commit.* 〉  (**D**)

**E**  Turpin's life even inspired a romantic musical!

# Questions

**1** What impression do you have of the real Dick Turpin?

**2** Which of the sources **A–E** are unreliable and why?

3 Which of the following statements about Turpin's life are supported by reliable evidence? **a** 'Turpin was the son of a butcher'; **b** 'Turpin was handsome and brave'; **c** 'Turpin once shot a man in self-defence'; **d** 'Turpin accidentally shot his friend, Tom King'; **e** 'Turpin rode to York on Black Bess'; **f** 'Turpin went to the gallows in 1739'.

4 Look through the sources again after reading the following known facts about Turpin's life.

> ❝Richard Turpin (1706–1739) was born at Hempstead, Essex, and executed at York. He was a farmer's son and became an apprentice in the butchery trade in Whitechapel, London. He went into business at Waltham Abbey and married an innkeeper's daughter, Hester Palmer. To impove his business prospects, he started stealing cattle and cutting them up for sale. He later became a poacher and housebreaker. From 1735 onwards he took to highway robbery. In 1739 he was found guilty of horse-stealing and was sentenced to death by hanging.❞

**a** (Which description (**1**, **2** or **3**) do you now think describes Turpin best? Has your opinion changed since you answered question **1**?

**b** How does Turpin's own account of his life, **D**, confirm the known facts about the highwayman?

5 Why do you think Mr Thompson's servant (**D**) was so keen to capture or kill Turpin?

6 Use **C** to design a 'Wanted' poster for Turpin.

7 Dick Turpin's name has been remembered in history while the names of hundreds of other thieves and highwaymen have been forgotten. Can you think why? You could mention: books, plays, films, TV programmes, pop singers, mythology.

# 2  Turpike riot

In the early eighteenth century most roads in Britain were in very poor condition. Better roads were essential if the economy was to expand. Part of the answer seemed to lie in the introduction of toll-roads or 'turnpikes'. Between 1700 and 1750 the government passed over 50 Turnpike Acts permitting merchants and businessmen to form turnpike trusts to organise the building and repair of roads. They charged people a small fee or toll for travelling along the road.

Not everyone was keen on the idea of turnpike trusts. Some people objected to paying for what had once been free and 'turnpike riots' took place in some parts of the country. **A** describes the riots which took place near Bristol in 1749.

*❝ **Bristol, 29th July**. On Monday 24th July, at night, great numbers of Somerset people destroyed the turnpike gates near Bedminster on the Ashton road. The trustees offered a reward of £100 to the discovery of any persons concerned therein, or in any future act of that kind, besides His Majesty's pardon. On July 25 at night, a body of Gloucestershire people, some naked with only trousers, some in their shirts, some naked with their faces blackened, destroyed a second time the turnpike gates and house at St John's Cross, about a mile from the city. They bored holes in the large posts and blew them up with gunpowder.*

*Cross-bars and gates were again put up and chains put across the roads, and men placed to assist the tollmen, and the trustees took it by turns, about a dozen in a body, to stand at the gates also, to awe the people and oblige them to pay the toll. Several persons, however, attempted to force their passage with cattle and colts for our fair and insulted the gentlemen. On the 26th July between ten and eleven at night, a huge number of Somerset people came with drums beating and loud shouts, armed with cutting instruments fixed in long staves and led by one, Jack Lent. Some were disguised in women's clothing and demolished the turnpike gates newly fixed, and the house rebuilding on the Ashton road, and the turnpike on the Dundry road.*

*On the 29th July, the turnpike gate was again erected on the Ashton road and guarded with a body of sailors, well armed with muskets, pistols and cutlasses. A body of gentlemen led by Sir Henry Browne made an excursion 8 miles into Somerset, took one of the rioters at Backwell, and brought him pinioned behind one of their servants to Bedminster.*

***Bristol, Tuesday 1st August**. At eight o'clock in the morning, about 400 Somerset people cut down a third time the turnpike gates on the Ashton road and burnt the timber; then afterwards destroyed the Dundry turnpike and thence to Bedminster, headed by two chiefs on horseback, one, with his face covered, on a black horse with a white star, and the other a young gentleman farmer at Nailsey carried the standard, being a silk handkerchief on a long staff; the rest were on* foot armed with rusty swords, pitchforks, axes, guns, pistols and clubs. They called themselves Jack a Lents, having the letters 'JL' on their hats and caps. They ranged themselves in the main street before the George Inn, by beat of a drum, huzzas, and a hunting horn, three drums attending them.

**Bristol, Thursday 3rd August**. The people in Kingswood kept gathering, and parties of them finished what the Somerset people had left undone, so that almost all the turnpikes and turnpike houses about the city were destroyed. The rioters, who numbered more than 700, insisted on the release of all prisoners, as a condition of them returning to their homes, threatening otherwise to deliver them up by force.

**Bristol, Friday 4th August**. About midnight, the colliers, as they had threatened the day before, came to Stokecross with loud huzzas and partly cut down that turnpike. Notice being given by signals and the clanging of fire bells, a large body of gentlemen and citizens well armed, with some soldiers and sailors, marched to the attack. The colliers did not stay to receive them.

**Bristol, Saturday 5th August**. Seven Kingswood rioters were taken in a brief struggle by a body of sailors employed to guard the turnpikes. One, Robert Price, was committed to Ilchester Gaol, for heading a gang of rioters to destroy the turnpikes – on the 6th August, Fitzharding, Pierce, Robins and two others were sent to gaol for the same offence. But it is said that these were not the real ring leaders.

**Bristol, Saturday 12th August**. By the arrival of six troops of dragoon guards on the 6th August, we are now secured from all the insults and disorderly conduct of the country people who have disgraced themselves by their late action. All the country people are now soundly dispersed and posts and chains erected and tolls levied. But now the turnpikes are fixed nearer the city. ❜ (**A**)

(*The Gentleman's Magazine*, 1749)

# Questions

**1** Read through the evidence in **A**. List or summarise the events which occurred on each day.
   **a** Why did the riots take place?
   **b** How were the riots stopped?
   **c** What effects do you think the riots had on the social and economic life of the community?

**2** In September 1749, a Commission of Enquiry was held into the riots. What evidence would have been given to the Commission? Take one of the roles (**B**) and write out the evidence you might have given if you had been present at the enquiry or, in the case of the commissioners, what you think are the most important facts of the case. The horse dealer's evidence (**C**) and the beggar's evidence (**D**) are set out as examples. These two pieces of evidence will be used during the hearing.

**B**  People involved in the Commission enquiry

| **Five Commissioners** (including one Chief Commissioner) to put questions to witnesses. | | |
| --- | --- | --- |
| THE WITNESSES | | |
| **Sir Henry Browne** | : | age 60; the local squire; owns estates in Somerset and Devon; walks with a slight limp, local people say it's gout. |
| **A reporter for *The Gentleman's Magazine*** | : | has travelled down from London; university background; his father edits the paper. |
| **A gentleman farmer** | : | age 48; farms at Lower Knowle, near Bristol; in favour of turnpikes because he believes they will help agriculture. |
| **Toll-keeper** at Ashton Gate | : | formerly employed in the docks. |
| **Toll-keeper** at St John's Cross | : | formerly employed in a foundry. |
| THE MILITARY | | |
| **A dragoon officer** | : | age 25; bought his commission; eldest son of a Gloucestershire landowner; lives in London. |
| **A naval officer** | : | age 36, from *HMS Endurance* in Bristol Dock; seafaring background; father a Rear Admiral. |
| **A soldier** | : | from Bristol barracks; a volunteer; had been in army 12 years; fought at Dettingen against the French. |
| **A sailor** | : | from *HMS Endurance*; pressed into service in 1747; not happy about life in navy. |

---

THE ANTI-TURNPIKE GROUP

**A collier** : from Radstock Colliery; on low wages; age 30, looks 40.

**Robert Price** : leader of rioters, 5th August; farm labourer from Dundry, near Bristol; has large family; on low wages.

**John Harding** : farm labourer from Bedminster; currently out of work.

**Susannah Pierce** : wife of a collier, age 28, no children.

**Susan Robins** : daughter of a hand-loom weaver; lives at home with her father; age 23; one child; father going blind; low income.

**A gentleman farmer** : age 42; from Nailsey; owns 120 acres; believes turnpikes are bad for agriculture.

---

OTHER WITNESSES

**A shepherd** : witnessed the riots on 29th July and 1st August; has lived in Bristol area all his life; resents paying 5d every time he wishes to take livestock along a turnpike road.

**A horse-dealer** (See **C.**) : hires out horses in the city; age 36.

**A pedlar** : travels round the West Country selling lace, ribbons, yarn; finds toll-gates inconvenient and expensive.

**A beggar** (See **D.**) : lost his job on a farm at Ashton in 1744; partially disabled as a result of falling under a wagon in 1745; always keen to pick up snippets of information.

---

❝ *Horse-dealer's evidence: 'I own two stables along West Street, Bedminster. I do a fair bit of trade with travellers in these parts, renting out the odd hack and gig, and buying and selling horses. You don't make a great deal of money like this, but it's a living. On the night of August 1st, I had a black stallion brought in by a well-spoken man with a slight limp. He said he wanted to sell the horse quickly as he needed money to pay off gambling debts. The strange thing is that he sold me the horse far too cheaply – below half its market value. It was as if he wanted to get rid of the horse at any price. The horse had a white star on its head.* **(C)**

**Beggar's evidence:** *'I lost my job five years ago; the farmer I worked for said I drank too much. Since then I have travelled the highways of Somerset searching for employment. Since the introduction of the turnpikes my movements have been restricted. It's been much harder finding work or alms. On Saturday 23rd July 1749, I was seeking alms from the houses occupied by the wealthier citizens of Bristol in the Bedminster area. As I left one house, I noticed a black horse being led away from the stables by two men. The horse was heavily laden with saddlebags; one of the men was hooded. He had the initials JL on his hood. As far as I know the house was owned by a knight as the servants made several references to 'The Dun Knight'. As I was leaving I saw a man approach the two men with the horse. He had a slight limp.*

*As for all these riotous assemblies at the toll-gates, I have kept clear of them.* **(D)**

**3** In class, the commissioners should lead the trial and 'witnesses' should read out their evidence. The witnesses should follow the rules set out below (**E**). The session should begin after the Chief Commissioner has read out the preamble (**F**). The class should come to a decision about who instigated (started) the riot after all the witnesses have been heard.

**1** It is assumed that all witnesses were in the Bristol area 24th July – 12th August.

**2** All witnesses must tell the truth!

**3** Commissioners are not allowed to ask **direct questions**, e.g. 'Were you responsible?', 'Are you guilty?', etc. They can only question the witnesses as to the events that took place.

**4** The commissioners have been unable to trace 'Jack Lent'.

**5** Each witness will be required to read a short statement; the commissioners, having heard the statement, can then question the witness if they so wish.

**E** Rules relating to Commission of Enquiry

This Commission is being held to determine the reasons for the untimely and untoward events which took place in and around the city of Bristol in July and August 1749.

It is not a court of law and has no legal powers. A number of witnesses will be called before the commissioners to read a short statement. The commissioners may then ask the witnesses questions if they so wish. The findings of this Commission may be referred to the Crown's legal advisers in due course.

Here are the facts as they stand ... [*read out the most important facts*]

In a moment the witnesses will be called to give their evidence as to what happened during this turbulent week.

**F** Preamble to be read by Chief Commissioner

**4** Sir Henry was finally acquitted (declared innocent) of the charges (**G**). Why had he been accused of inciting the rioters? What had he to gain? Some people believed that he had started the riot in order to discredit the local farmers and businessmen who were strongly against the introduction of the turnpike system! What do you think?

❢ *On Tuesday 4th September, Sir Henry Browne was tried by jury at Bristol Crown Court for 'inciting a number of ill-designing and disorderly persons to associate themselves both by day and night and encouraging them to cut down, pull down, burn down or otherwise destroy several toll-houses and gates'.*

*The case against Sir Henry collapsed after one hour when two key witnesses failed to appear before the court.*

*The body of one witness, Samuel Knowles, horse-dealer, was subsequently discovered on the lower reaches of the River Avon. It was assumed that he had fallen into the river accidentally and his body had been washed downstream.*

*The other witness, Henry Wilkins, a vagrant, was never traced.*

*Sir Henry was acquitted of all the charges against him.* ❢ (**G**)

# 3 Roads in Devon

Maps **A** and **B** show the same part of Devon in 1765 and 1986. Study the maps and then answer these questions.

EXPLANATION.

Turnpike Roads or intended to be made such.

Inclosed Roads.

Open Roads over Commons or Downs.

Roads open on one side with a hedge on the other.

**A** Devon, 1765

**B** Devon, 1986

# Questions

**1** Look at the map of 1765. What symbols do you think were used for: a church; a large house; high ground; an unfenced road? What symbols would be used for these on a modern map?

**2** On the 1765 map, what do you think the letters and numbers (eg E 6 Ott) stand for?

**3** In 1765 who lived at: **a** Bystock; **b** Bicton Lodge; **c** Treasurer's bere; **d** Higher House?

**4 a** On the old map, how are the turnpike roads marked in?
  **b** What happened to the turnpike road between St Mary's Clyst and Newton Poppleford? How do you explain this?

**5** Find six places which have the same names on both maps.

  **b** Write down six places whose names have changed in some way.

  **c** What problems do such changes create for the historian?

**6** In which areas does there seem to have been most development 1765–1986? How do you explain this?

**7 a** What are the most obvious mistakes on the old map? You can assume that the modern map is 98% accurate.

  **b** Can you think of one reason why it was difficult for eighteenth century cartographers to make very accurate maps?

**8** It is the year 1765. You are a fisherman from Exmouth. You decide to take a packhorse loaded with shellfish and herrings from Exmouth to St George's Clyst. You sell some herrings at St George's Clyst and then ride on to St Mary's Clyst. You then ride back to Exmouth via East Budley where you pick up some cloth and vegetables.

Using the old map and the new map, describe your journey in detail. You should mention: turnpike roads (probably in reasonable condition); open roads (possibly in poor condition); houses, villages, churches, people you see on your journey; hills (see modern map); the appearance of the countryside (mainly enclosed fields in this part of Devon in 1765).

# 4  Canal mania

The map over the page shows two towns, Borchester and Wadham, in the year 1770. The aim of the game is to build a canal from Borchester to Wadham which will make a profit. Each round you can build your canal a certain distance in any direction according to the toss of a coin. The scale of the map is $\frac{1}{2}$ cm to 1 mile.

**1 Preparation**. Divide yourselves up into groups of four for each 'company'. Make up a name for your canal company. Appoint a treasurer who will do the sums; an engineer who will build the

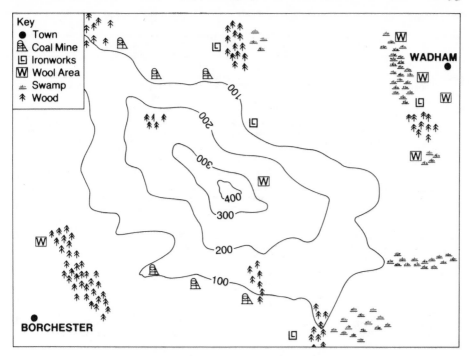

canal; a director who will make important decisions; a secretary who will write down what happens each round.

2 **Planning.** Work out the route of your canal in pencil. The canal will cost your company £1 000 per mile. Every time you cross a contour line or go across a swamp ( ) or wood ( ), the cost per mile is doubled. If your canal goes through a coal mine ( ), ironworks ( ) or wool area ( ), the cost for that mile is halved.

3 **Costs.** Work out the cost of building your canal. You may need a bit extra for emergencies. If you go bankrupt (run out of money) while the canal is being built, you may not be able to complete the canal. When you know how much the canal is going to cost your company, go to the bank (the teacher) and ask for a loan. The amount you borrow will be noted down by the bank. Interest will be charged at 10%. If, for example, you borrow £20 000, the interest you pay back at the end will be £2 000.

4 **Playing.** Each company will toss a coin to see what happens each round. If, for example, you throw 'heads' in round one you can build three miles of canal; your engineer can then mark in three miles (1½ cm) in any direction in red ink. Your treasurer should keep a running total of how much money you have left.

5 **The winner.** The winning company is the group which chooses the best route and builds the canal at the lowest cost. At the end of the game, tell the bank how much money you have left over.

| Round | Heads | Tails |
|---|---|---|
| 1 | James Brindley gives you some good advice this round. Build three miles but pay for two! | Work is going well on your canal. Build two miles but pay for one! |
| 2 | The price of engineering equipment has fallen. Build two miles but pay only £100 towards construction. | The navvies' camp is flooded by a freak rainstorm. Miss a go. |
| 3 | Fire breaks out in the navvies' camp! You pay £500 to replace their huts. Build one mile. | Canal-building is going well. Two local coal-owners send you £1 000 for your canal and you build two miles. |
| 4 | An ironmaster has let you have a supply of water from a forge pool. Build three miles. | You have to build an aqueduct this round. Build one mile of canal but pay for four miles. |
| 5 | Your navvies have got drunk! Miss a round. | If the route of your canal passes through a farm, a coal mine or an ironworks, build three miles this round. Otherwise build one mile. |
| 6 | Good news! 45 navvies come to work on your canal and you build three miles this round. | Navvies go on strike! Miss a turn. |
| 7 | Disaster! Slight earth tremor and loss of water in the canal. Miss a go and pay £100 to line the bed of the canal. | The navvies are working very hard at the moment. Build three miles this round. |
| 8 | Your canal is making good progress. Build two miles. | A local landowner objects to you building over his land. Build two miles but pay an extra £500 to 'buy him off'. |
| 9 | Murder! A navvy has stabbed a farm worker in a village pub. This holds up work. Build half a mile this round. | Weather fine, subsoil sound, navvies working hard. Build three miles this round. |
| 10 | Light, sandy soil makes canal-building easy. Build two miles this round. | Bad news! The mile of canal you build this round costs you twice as much as you expect. |
| 11 | You are forced to build a lock this round. Build one mile of canal but pay for two. | Plenty of water for canal from local streams. Build two miles this round. |
| 12 | If the route of your canal passes through a coal mine, build three miles. If not, build one mile. | Six navvies killed in an explosion. You will have to pay out £600 in compensation. Build two miles this round. |
| 13 | Two canal directors quarrel and one goes off in a rage. Build only half a mile this round. | Good news! Everything is going extremely well. Build four miles this round. |
| 14 | Thomas Telford comes to your canal. He explains how to build four miles of canal for the cost of two. | Your canal freezes over this round. Miss a go. |
| 15 | High winds and sleet hold up building the canal. Build only half a mile this turn. | Good weather for canal building. Build four miles this round. |
| 16 | If the route of your canal passes through an ironworks, accept a gift of £1 000 from an ironmaster and build three miles. If not, no extra money and one mile. | Drought! The water in your canal is drying up. Miss a turn. |
| 17 | Local landowners hostile to canal building smash up the workings. Miss a turn. | Plenty of raw materials near your canal. Build three miles this turn. |
| 18 | Navvies working hard! Build three miles! | Landslip! Miss a turn. |
| 19 | Thunderstorm! Floods mean you build only half a mile. | Local people help with digging the canal. Build two miles this round. |
| 20 | Sir Francis Harwood sends you £5 000 towards the cost of your canal. Build five miles! | Good news! A local wool merchant has sent you £4 000 towards the cost of your canal. Build four miles. |

# 5   The Canal Bill

❝ Come, now begin _delving_, the Bill is obtained,
The contest was hard, but a conquest is gained;
Let no time be lost, and to get business done,
Set thousands to work, that will work down the sun.

With speed the desirable work to complete,
The hope how _alluring_ – the spirit how great!
By Severn we soon, I've no doubt in my mind,
With old Father Thames shall an _intercourse_ find.

By int'rested motives tho' people are led,
With many the ground who they fancy may tread;
'Twill _prejudice_ stifle, and _malice_ strike dumb,
When the seat of the Arts shall a seaport become.

Redditch, where the sons of the Needle reside,
Who commerce _revere_, and make friendship their pride,
The prospect _enraptures_ – and Bromsgrove no less,
Has cause at the victory joy to express.

In Europe's grand toy-shop how pleasing 'twill be,
Well freighted with _trows_, and the barges to see;
The country 'twill charm, and new life give to trade,
When the seat of the Arts shall a seaport be made.

With _pearmains_ and _pippins_ 'twill gladden the _throng_,
Full loaded the boats to see floating along;
And fruit that is fine, and good hops for our ale,
Like Wednesbury pit-coal will always find sale.

So much does the rage for canals seem to grow,
That vessels accustom'd to Bristol to go;
Will soon be deserting the Severn's fair tide,
For shallows and shoals sailors wish to avoid.

As freedom I prize, and my country respect,
I trust not a soul to my toast will object;
'Success to the plough, not forgetting the spade,
Health, plenty and peace, navigation and trade. ❞   (A)

(A song, on obtaining the Birmingham and Worcester Canal Bill, 1791.
Author not known, but possibly John Freeth.)

*❝It is with great pleasure we announce to the public, the progress of the Worcester and Birmingham canal, which, on Monday 30 March, was opened from Hopwood to Tardebig, an extension of nearly five miles. On that day a number of vessels arrived at the wharf of Tardebig, laden with more than 300 tons of coals, most part of which was immediately sold on such terms as to insure a continued supply of that invaluable article. This must prove of vast importance to the Owners of Coal Mines communicating with that canal. We now foresee with pleasure the conclusion of this important work ... which renders the carriage of goods between the port of Bristol and Birmingham certain, cheap and speedy.❞*  (B)

(From *The Times*, 11 April 1807)

Map **C** shows central Britain's canal and river systems in 1790.

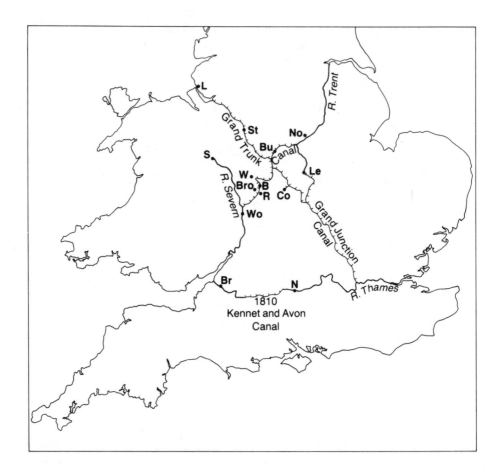

**C**  Canals and rivers in 1790

# Questions

1 Match up the letters in the map (C) with the following places: Birmingham; Bristol; Wednesbury; Newbury; Coventry; Leicester; Nottingham; Burton; Stoke; Liverpool; Shrewsbury; Redditch; Bromsgrove; Worcester. For example, 'Br' stands for Bristol.

2 A list of synonyms (a–k) is printed below. Try matching them up with the words underlined in the song. For example, delving in the song means digging. a digging; b two varieties of apple; c respect; d tempting, attractive; e communication; f crowd of people; g delights; h ill-will, bad feeling; j preconceived idea, bias; k river vessels.

3 Use the map and the song to work out:
a where 'Europe's grand toy-shop' was;
b which goods were carried on the Birmingham and Worcester Canal;
c which river formed part of the Birmingham–Worcester waterway;
d how Birmingham was eventually linked to the River Thames and London as a result of the Birmingham-Worcester Canal.

4 Explain what the following lines in the song mean.
a 'Set thousands to work, that will work down the sun.'
b 'Success to the plough, not forgetting the spade,
Health, plenty and peace, navigation and trade.'

5 a The canal bill was passed in 1791. Is there any evidence in *The Times* extract (B) to suggest that the canal had not been completed by 1807?
b How would people living in the West Midlands have benefited from the new canal? You could mention: cheaper goods; canal towns; wages; jobs; investments. (Refer to other history textbooks if possible.)

# 6 Railway disaster!

❝ *The railway will cause wholesale destruction of human life. No doubt people will be pleased to learn that they are in no danger of being seasick while they are on shore, that they are not to be scalded to death or drowned by the bursting of a boiler, and that they need not mind being shot by the scattered fragments or dashed in pieces by the flying off of a wheel. But will they believe it?* ❞ **(A)**

(*The Quarterly*, 1825)

❝ *It was declared that the railway would prevent cows from grazing and hens laying. The poisonous air from the locomotive would kill birds as they flew over and kill off pheasants and foxes. Householders living close to the line were told that their houses would be burnt up by the fire thrown from the engine chimneys; while the air around would be polluted by clouds of smoke. There would no longer be any use for horses and if the railways caught on, the species would become extinct. No one would be able to sell oats and hay.* ❞ **(B)**

(Samuel Smiles, *The Lives of George and Robert Stephenson*, 1857)

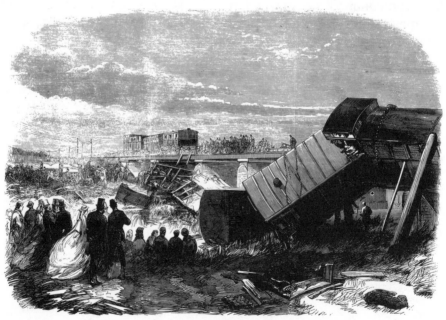

**C** Artist's impression of the June 1865 disaster

❝On June 9, 1865 on the South Eastern Railway, the 'Tidal' boat train from Folkestone was wrecked in a most dramatic manner . . . Near Staplehurst the line crosses a small stream called the Beult on a low bridge. In June 1865 this bridge was the site of a track repair which involved renewing some of the bridge timbers. It involved taking out the rails and replacing the timber baulks (beams) with new ones. The foreman and his gang knew all about the Tidal boat train and its variation in time from day to day; but on the last day, when one more baulk would have seen the job completed, the foreman looked up the wrong date . . . after the previous train had gone and the signals had been replaced to 'clear', he and his men got to work, removed the rails and set about replacing the timbers beneath.

Very soon after they had begun work and the rails were removed, up came the Tidal boat train at full speed. The driver got the warning from the look-out man but it was not enough. The man was much too close to the bridge and with the ineffective brakes then in use there was not a hope of the train being able to stop. The train came to the gap in the rails, crashed down onto the iron girders of the bridge and ploughed its way along. The engine and the first two carriages got across to the far side and came to rest on the ballast on the embankment. But the couplings broke between the second and third carriages.❞ **(D)**

(O S Nock, *Historic Railway Disasters*, 1966)

❝I was on the only carriage that did not go over into the stream. It was caught upon the turn by some of the ruins of the bridge and hung suspended in an impossible manner. Two ladies were my fellow passengers . . . suddenly we were off the rail and beating the ground as the car of a half-emptied balloon might . . . We were then all tilted down together in a corner of the carriage (which was locked) and stopped . . . I got out through the window without the least idea of what had happened . . . with great caution and stood upon the step . . . looking down I saw the bridge gone and nothing below me but the line of rail. There was nothing else. I saw all the rest of the train except the two baggage vans, down in the stream . . . No imagination can conceive the ruin of the carriages.❞ **(E)**

(Charles Dickens' account of the June 9 disaster, 1865)

❝I would like to give you an account of the sad railway accident on the line on June 9, when 10 persons were killed and many wounded and disabled. It was indeed a fearful affair. I was on the spot soon after the crash and saw six bodies taken out dead and others severely mangled. The sufferers have been lying at different houses in the village. They were chiefly persons of good circumstances returning *in the boat train from the Continent and every care was taken of them. The last sufferer, Major Thorpe, has only just left us.* **(F)**

(Letter from Mrs Ethel Mann to her great grandfather William Jull on
August 17, 1865)

## Questions

**1 a** Which of sources **A–F** are secondary?
**b** Place **A–F** in their correct chronological order.
**c** List six reasons mentioned in **A** and **B** which help to explain why some people opposed the early railways. Do you think any of these objections were valid? Why?

**2 a** How do extracts **D**, **E** and **F** confirm what is shown in **C**?
**b** Which of the written sources appears to contradict what is shown in **C**?

**3** How was railway safety improved during the nineteenth century? You could mention: speed; time; signalling; rules; rails; locomotives; carriages; brakes; civil engineering. (You need to refer to other history books to answer this.)

# 7   The transport revolution

*In years to come it is likely that we may see the roads all over England improved so much that travelling and the sending of goods will be much easier both to man and horse . . . The waggoners and pack-horse drivers will either make their journeys in less time or carry heavier loads, or the same load with fewer horses. All this will bring goods cheaper to market. The fat cattle will go further in a day and not waste their flesh and heat and spoil themselves, in wandering through the mud and bogs. The sheep will also be able to travel in winter and fresh mutton will be sold to the people of London all the year round.* **❯** (A)

(Arthur Young, *A Tour Through the Whole Island of Great Britain*, 1727)

**❮** *Instead of being covered in miserable thatch, cottages are now covered with tiles or slates brought from Wales or Cumberland. The fields which used to be barren are now drained; by covering them with manure, carried on the canal toll-free, they have become green and fertile. Places which rarely obtained coal now have plentiful, cheap supplies. The corn merchants are prevented from charging high prices because a line of communication has been opened up between Bristol and Hull. This canal, being through counties of abundant grain, makes the carrying of corn easier than in past ages.* **❯** (B)

(Thomas Pennant, *A Treatise on Inland Navigation*, 1782)

**❮** *There were railway patterns in the drapers' shops and railway journals in the windows of newsmen. There were railway hotels, office houses, lodging houses, boarding houses; railway plans, maps, views, wrappers, bottles, sandwich boxes, timetables; railway hackney coaches and cabstands; railway omnibuses; railway streets and buildings, railway hangers-on . . .*

*There were crowds of people and mountains of goods departing and arriving, scores upon scores of times every day. Night and day, the conquering engines rumbled at their distant work, gliding like tame dragons into the corners grooved out for them. They stood bubbling and trembling, making the wall quake, as if they were shivering with the secret knowledge of great powers within them and strong purposes not yet achieved.* **❯** (C)

(Charles Dickens, *Dombey and Son*, 1847)

**❮** *The revolution in transport brought great changes in British social and economic life. The railways were chiefly responsible, but only because of their greater scale and scope.*

*The economic consequences may be divided into five main groups. There were important results for industry as a whole. More goods were transported more quickly and more cheaply to wider markets . . . Secondly, there were particular benefits for some industries. The heavy industries, notably iron, received a great impetus . . . Agriculture gained much for it was now possible to send perishable goods a long distance. The agricultural changes of the nineteenth century owed much to the Transport Revolution. Even fishing gained . . . There were large gains for Britain's overseas trade. This was speeded up by quicker transport to and from the ports. The Transport Revolution also created new job opportunities . . . Lastly, there were some important effects of the vast sums of money spent on transport development. Much was done to improve the financial institutions of the country . . .*

*On the social side the standard of living was improved in three main ways. First, the cheapening of goods, especially food had an important effect. Better diets must have aided the falling death-rates, especially among infants . . . Second, there were many benefits from the easier spread of newspapers, mail and electric telegraph. Third, many ordinary people gained for the first time from being able to travel beyond their own district.*

*All this meant that the revolution in transport helped to break down the limited horizons of the majority of people in the country. Easier travel made Britain much more of a nation.*' **(D)**

(M St J Parker & D J Reid, *The British Revolution 1750–1970*, 1972)

| | |
|---|---|
| 1766 – 12 days | 1830 – $1\frac{1}{2}$ days |
| 1776 – 4 days | 1890 – 9 hours |
| 1796 – $2\frac{1}{2}$ days | 1989 – $4\frac{1}{2}$ hours |

**E** Journey times (by road and rail) between London and Edinburgh 1766–1989 (400 miles)

# Questions

**1** Which of the sources **A–E** mention: **a** food; **b** employment; **c** investment; **d** the social effects of improved transport?

**2 a** How do sources **A–D** help to explain the statistics in **E**?
**b** Which forms of transport do you think were used to measure the journey times 1766–1989 (**E**)?

**3** 'Sources **A** and **B** are primary sources written by eighteenth century travellers; **C** is from a novel by Dickens. **A** and **B** are therefore more useful sources of information than **C**.' Do you agree with this statement? Give reasons for your answer.

**4 a** What opposition was there to the methods of transport mentioned in **A–D**?
**b** Why do you think new forms of transport attracted so much criticism?

**5** Which method of transport mentioned in **A–D** would you say had the greatest impact on the social and economic life of the nation? Give reasons for your answer.

# 8   Motor transport

❝'Mary,' cried the landlord of the Duke's Arms to his wife. 'It's wonderful! Here's life and hope coming back to the old house – in motor cars. Just think of it, five of 'em stopped here today and we served fourteen meals. Never mind if they do smell different from horses. New life, business – coming back.'

'Yes, John, and now stop talking and start working,' replied his very much better half. These new folk will expect clean table-cloths and new cutlery . . . good beds and blankets and sheets . . . And another thing. These people will want motor spirit instead of hay and corn. The stables aren't much use, but the coach house can be turned into a . . . what's the French word, John? There seems to be a lot of French in this new business.'

'It's garage, Mary. I saw it in one of the new motor papers.❞ **(A)**

(Sir Stenson Cooke, *This Motoring*, 1931)

❝Lord Carnarvon is becoming a public nuisance as a motor scorcher. Clouds of dust as high as the neighbouring trees, said the police witness, rose up as his car whizzed along the road. By careful timing and measurement the superintendent calculated the speed at a mile in two and a half minutes, or 24 miles an hour.❞ **(B)**

(R D Blumenfeld, *Diary*, 1900)

| Description of traffic | 15 July, 1903 | 31 July, 1904 |
|---|---|---|
| 2 wheeled carts | 812 | 642 |
| 4 wheeled carts and hansoms | 2 371 | 2 574 |
| Buses (horse-drawn) | 5 443 | 5 707 |
| Cycles | 1 090 | 867 |
| Motor Cars, private | 33 | 272 |
| Motor Cars, commercial | 16 | 85 |
| Foot passengers | 51 610 | 62 370 |

**C**   Traffic census at Strand, by the Law Courts 8 am to 12 pm

❝As for motors, jest cast yer eye over that blinkin' arrangement! Cross between a pram and a steam-roller; give me a horse any day of the week. This off-side un's a bit of a jibber, but when 'e drops unexpected 'e don't need an engin' driver to start 'im again . . . Ah *well Sir, the business will last out my time, and then I'll make way for the lady drivers and motor-buses and wot not.* **(D)**

(Interview with a horse-bus driver, October 19, 1904)

*I bought a Riley. It could manage up to 35 to 40 miles per hour. I sold it before I left Sidmouth, and with the trusting purchaser's cheque in my pocket, took him for a spin; we spoke of 'spins' in those far off days. We were cruising down the main road of Wellington in Somerset when, before anything could be done about it, I noticed a small open drain, about two inches deep and six inches wide, running across the road. On crossing it, perhaps doing 40 miles an hour, both the front wheels came off at the same time, the car came to its knees with an abrupt jerk and slid some yards along the road. In spite of this disaster my friend kept the car and I the cheque, despite a small repair bill . . .* **(E)**

(Roger Eckersley, *The BBC and All That*, 1946)

**F** Traffic at Piccadilly Circus, 1910

# Questions

**1** Explain what is meant by the following: **a** 'There seems to be a lot of French in this new business'; **b** 'A motor scorcher'; **c** 'Hansoms'; **d** 'This off-side un's a bit of a jibber'; **e** 'Took him for a spin'.

**2 a** How reliable are the statistics in **C**?
   **b** Why do you think the traffic census was taken?
   **c** What trends do the statistics show?

**3** Use different sources to explain the social and economic effects of the introduction of motor transport in the early twentieth century.

# Section IV
# LAW AND ORDER

# 1 Breakout!

---

**11<sup>th</sup> MAY, 1761.**

## Broke out of his Majefty's Goal,

At *Wilton*, near *Taunton*, in the County of *Somerfet* ;
in the Night, between the *Nineteenth* and *Twentieth*
Days of *April* laft, with two other Prifoners fince
Re-taken,

## GEORGE PEARSE ;

Committed for Returning from Tranfportation before
the Time limited.

THE faid GEORGE PEARSE is about fixty Years Old, and five
Feet five Inches High ; has a large Face ; a flat Mouth,
which, when he Speaks, is drawn rather to one fide of his Face.
He has loft all his fore Teeth, and ftammers in his Speech ;
leans very forward in Walking ; his Legs bending outwards ; has
Black Hair, which hangs loofe about his Ears : Speaks Lifping,
and had on (when he went away) an old Blue Coat, Leather
Breeches, and White Stockings.———He pretends to be a Farrier,
and to underftand and Cure Diforders in *Bullocks* and *Sheep* ; and
generally carries with him fome Papers, fhowing what Cures he
pretends to have Wrought on Cattle.

HE was born at *Withypoole*, in the County aforefaid.

Whoever Re-takes and Secures the faid GEORGE PEARSE, (fo
as he may be brought back again to the faid Goal) fhall receive
*Three Guineas* Reward, with all Reafonable Expences, of GEORGE
STRONG, Keeper of the faid Goal ; and all Magiftrates and Peace-
Officers, are earneftly defired to Search for the faid Delinquent,
in their feveral Precinfts.

*NORTON*, near *TAUNTON:* Printed by I. PILE.

**A**  'Wanted' poster for George Pearse

## Questions

**1 a** Which prison had George Pearse (**A**) escaped from?
  **b** When did he escape?
  **c** How many prisoners had escaped with him?
  **d** Why had Pearse been put in prison?

e How much was the reward for his recapture in modern currency?
(1 guinea=£1.05)
f In which county is Withypoole?

**2 a** Is there any evidence to suggest what Pearse's occupation was?
**b** Why do you think the authorities waited three weeks before publishing the notice?
**c** There seems to be a serious spelling error made repeatedly on the notice. What is it?

**3 a** Using the information on the poster, tell the story of George Pearse in your own words.
**b** How would a modern 'Wanted' poster issued by the police differ from this eighteenth century poster?

# 2 Resurrection men

In the late eighteenth century doctors and surgeons needed dead human bodies for medical research. Dissection (cutting up dead bodies) was illegal and so surgeons had to buy corpses illegally from grave robbers or 'resurrection men'. The grave robbers would visit a graveyard shortly after a burial, dig up the coffin, remove the body and replace the soil. A skilled gang of robbers could do the whole job in less than an hour. They were paid as much as three guineas (£3.15) for each corpse which was the equivalent of several weeks' pay for an ordinary working man. The resurrection men were so unpopular that they ran the risk of being beaten to death if a mob caught them. Churchyards and graves were surrounded by huge iron railings. There were fewer grave robberies after 1745 when the Company of Surgeons was given a regular supply of bodies to dissect but in some places surgeons still ran short of bodies (**A**).

❛ Early on Tuesday morning, some suspicion being entertained that the Pesthouse burial ground, in Old Street, had been often violated, *the parish watchmen were ordered to keep a good look out, when a hackney coach was observed, waiting near the spot. Upon the watchman's approaching it, he was assaulted, and beaten, by three men who then made off; but afterwards, springing his rattle (sounding the alarm), the assistants took the coachman into custody, who had three sacks in his coach, two of them containing the body of a man each, and the other, three children. Several other bodies which had been dug up for the purpose of carrying away, were found under the wall of the burying ground; and, it is generally believed, that almost all the bodies buried there, for five weeks past, have been stolen, which, upon an average, must have been 15 per week. . . The hackney coachman, who admitted he was to have ten guineas (£10.50) for his night's work, was committed to the New Prison, Clerkenwell. This fellow, it seems, was hardened to his business; for, though put into the cage with the bodies he was carrying off, he slept so sound that it was with some difficulty he was awakened by the visit of a brother-whip, previous to his going before a magistrate.* (A)

(*The Times*, December 23 1796)

Source **B** consists of entries made in Joseph Naples' diary between Thursday 28 November and Tuesday 3 December 1811. Joseph Naples was a body-snatcher who operated in the West End of London between 1805 and 1812.

*Thursday 28 November. At night went out and got 3. Jack & me Hospital Crib, Danl & Bill to Harpers, Jack & me 1 big gates, sold 1 Taunton, 1 St Thomas's.*
*Friday 29 November. Intoxsicated all day: at night went out & got 5 Bunhill Row. Jack almost buried alive.*
*Saturday 30 November. Went to St Thomas's, came home and went to the play, came home. At 3 am got up and went to the Hospital Crib, got 5 large.*
*Sunday 1 December. Met at Jacks. Got 4 large, 1 small and 1 foetus. Took them all to the London.*
*Monday 2 December. Went to St Thomas's, sold the extremities. At night Tom & Bill got drunk in the Rockingham Arms. So drunk oblige to come home in a coach which prevented us going out to Harps.*
*Monday 3 December. At home all the day, at night met Jack to go to Harps, the moon at the full, could not go.* (B)

In August 1832 Parliament passed an Anatomy Act which made it possible for surgeons to obtain dead bodies legally. The gruesome activities of the resurrection men came to an end.

# Questions

**1 a** Why were corpses stolen from graveyards in the eighteenth and nineteenth centuries?
**b** Why were the body snatchers nicknamed 'resurrection men'?
**c** What event brought the activities of the resurrection men to an end?

**2 a** In what sense was the hackney coachman in **A** a 'hardened character'?
**b** Suggest reasons why the body-snatchers in **B** went in for such heavy drinking.
**c** Use **B** to write your own account of what you think Joseph Naples did on the weekend of 29 November–2 December 1811.

**3** Which source (**A** or **B**) would you describe as: **a** most interesting; **b** accurate; **c** useful for an historian studying crime in the late eighteenth and early nineteenth centuries? Give reasons for your choice(s).

# 3 The calendar of prisoners

# Questions

Look at **A**.

**1 a** Explain what is meant by these words: vagrant; alias; surety.
**b** In what year was the calendar published?

**2** Draw up a table like the one started below and fill in the missing information for all of the prisoners, 1–23. The first entry has been done for you.

| Number | Name | Age | Sex | Offence |
|--------|------|-----|-----|---------|
| 1 | James Kerton | 28 | M | Stealing two bundles of hay |
| 2 | | | | |

**3** Refer to the table you have just created.

   **a** How many men were committed?

   **b** How many women were sent to prison?

   **c** Calculate the average age of the prisoners.

   **d** How many offences were connected with vagrancy and the poor law?

   **e** How many offences involved theft? How many involved violence?

   **f** Which names appear twice on the calendar?

**4** Explain in your own words exactly what you think William James and William Denner had done wrong.

**5** Why do you think the 'Calendar of the Prisoners' was published?

**6** Today, which of the crimes mentioned in the 'Calendar of Prisoners' would be considered: **a** very serious; **b** fairly serious; **c** minor?

**A**  Calendar of prisoners, 1805

## CALENDAR OF THE PRISONERS

*From Ivelchester Gaol.*

| | |
|---|---|
| 1 JAMES KERTON, *Aged 28.* | Committed the 19th of January 1805, by John Turner, Clerk; charged with stealing two bundles of hay, the property of John Lax. |
| 2 THOMAS HANN, *Aged 58.* | Committed the 21st of January, by W. Phelips, Clerk; charged with leaving his wife and family, chargeable to the parish of Brympton. |
| 3 GEORGE DUNOLD, *Aged 52.* | Committed the 31st of January, by W. Hanning, Esq. charged for want of sureties in bastardy. |
| 4 SAMPSON ANSTICE, *Aged 13* | Committed the 6th of February, by F. J. H. Festing, Clerk; charged with stealing a quantity of hay, the property of Matthew Osborne. |
| 5 THOMAS JONES, *Aged 25.* | Committed the 10th of February, by W. Wollen, Clerk; charged with leaving his child chargeable to the parish of Saint Decumans. |
| 6 HANNAH COLLINS, *Aged 21.* | Committed the 20th of February, by W. H. Colston, Clerk; charged with stealing a quantity of sugar, brandy, and wine, the property of Robert White, Esq. |

7 MARY GOSLING,     Committed the 20th of February, by W. H.
    *Aged* 27.         Colston, Clk. charged with stealing two neck
                    handkerchiefs, value of two shillings, and div-
                    ers other articles, the property of Robert
                    White, Esq.

8 JOHN COMBES,      Committed the 4th of April, by W. Wight-
    *Aged* 50.         wick, Clerk; charged with assaulting James
                    Middleton.

## From Wilton Gaol.

9 WILLIAM DENNER,   Committed the Second of February 1805, by
    *Aged* 63.         John Brickdale, Esq. for refusing to give
                    security to the parish of Wiveliscombe, in
                    bastardy.

10 A WOMAN, *Vagrant,*  Committed the 11th of February, by E. Halli-
    *Name unknown,*    day, Esq. Sir John Trevelyan, and George
    *A Foreigner.*     Trevelyan, Clerk; for wandering abroad in
                    the parish of Nettlecombe, as a vagabond.

11 ELIZABETH ENGLISH, Committed the 16th of March, by John
    *Aged* 87.         Gale, Clerk; for want of sureties of the peace.

12 JAMES TUCKER,    Committed the 8th of April, by J. F. Warre,
    *Aged* 32.         Esq. and John Gale, Clerk; charged on the
                    oath of Matthew Bowen, on suspicion of fel-
                    oniously stealing one bundle of hay, contain-
                    ing one hundred weight, value three shillings,
                    his property.

## From Shepton-Mallet Gaol.

13 ROBERT WILLIAMS,   Committed the 28th of January 1805, by James
    *alias* THOMAS WILLIAMS,  Tooker, Esq. and J. Stephens, Clerk; charged
    *Aged* 22.         on the oath of Richard Welch, Edmund Laver,
    JAMES CHINNOCK,    and others, with feloniously stealing and
14 *alias* THOMAS BISHOP,  carrying away a quantity of ducks and geese,
    *Aged* 28.         the property of the said Richard Welch and
                    Edmund Laver.

15 JAMES HOLLEY,    Committed the 29th of January, by William
    *Aged* 60,         Ireland, Clk. charged on the oath of Benja-
                    min Ball, overseer of the poor of the parish
                    of Cloford, with running away and leaving his
                    wife and child chargeable to the said parish.

16 CHARLOTTE FUSSELL, Committed the 6th of February, by T. S.
      *Aged* 19. Champneys Esq. charged on the oath of
Jonathan Noad the Younger, on a strong
suspicion of having feloniously stolen, and
carried away about three yards of unfinished
brown mixture woollen cloth, the property of
Jonathan Noad the Elder.

17 JAMES WEARE, Committed the 28th of February, by Sir John
      *Aged* 25. Durbin, Knt. charged on the oath of John
May, overseer of the poor of the parish of
Minehead, with running away and leaving his
wife and child chargeable to the said parish.

18 JAMES EVANS, Committed the 12th of March, by John
      *Aged* 55. Turner, Clerk; charged on the oath of Edward
Batt, of Wedmore, on suspicion of having
feloniously stolen and carried away a quantity
of hay, his property.

19 ISAAC CHUBB, Committed the 16th of March, by W. H.
      *Aged* 24. Colston, Clerk; charged on oath, with having
feloniously stolen and carried away a quantity
of alder poles and underwood, the property
of George Messiter, Gentleman.

20 JAMES CAVILL, Committed the 21st of March, by A. A.
      *Aged* 42. Baker, L. L. D. for want of sureties to keep
the peace.

21 CHARLES SHEPPARD, Committed the 23rd of March, by William
      *Aged* 14. Ireland, Clerk; charged on the oath of George
Richardson, on suspicion of having together
with George Richards, feloniously stolen and
carried away a paper or parcel containing five
or six clasp knives, his property.

22 WILLIAM JAMES, Committed the 13th of April, by Francis
      *Aged* 28. Drake, Esq. for want of sureties to indemnify
the parish of Shepton-Mallet, in bastardy.

23 JAMES ABRAHAM, Committed the 19th of April, by John God-
      *Aged* 35. frey, Esq. for want of sureties to keep the
peace towards Robert Guy, of Wellow.—*Since
Bailed.*

# 4  Ilchester gaol

## Questions

**1** Read through **A**. Make a list of any words or phrases you do not understand. Look these words up in a dictionary.

**2 a** To whom did James Hillier send his petition?
 **b** Why had Hillier been sent to prison in the first place?
 **c** Why had Hillier been placed in double irons?
 **d** For how long was Hillier kept in double irons?
 **e** What action did Hillier want the 'Honourable House' to take?

**3** Look carefully at **B**.
 **a** Why did the artist describe Ilchester Gaol as a 'bastille'?
 **b** Describe the different forms of punishment shown in **B**.
 **c** Which punishment had James Hillier (**A**) been subjected to?
 **d** Do you think conditions were really this bad in Ilchester Gaol?
 **e** You are an influential MP in 1821 who has read James Hillier's petition. What do you think about the case? What action do you take?

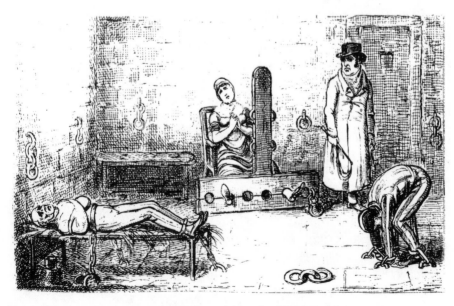

**B**  An artist's impression of life in Ilchester Bastille

TO THE HONOURABLE THE COMMONS OF THE UNITED KINGDOM
OF GREAT BRITAIN AND IRELAND, IN PARLIAMENT ASSEMBLED.

*The humble Petition of JAMES HILLIER, a Prisoner in his
Majesty's Gaol of Ilchester, in the county of Somerset.*

MOST HUMBLY SHEWETH,

That your petitioner is confined in his Majesty's gaol at Ilchester, under
a sentence of eighteen months, for stealing in a shop at Bristol; that some
time in the second week in February last your petitioner and another
prisoner were playing at hussel-cap for a few pence; that another prisoner,
confined for a similar offence (stealing), of the name of Penny, having
interfered, a squabble ensued, whereupon the said Penny reported your
petitioner to the Governor for having played at hussel-cap; upon which
your petitioner was immediately placed in heavy double irons, twice
doubled, so that he could not move his legs more than nine inches apart:
handcuffs were then placed upon him, and a chain passed from the fetters
through the handcuffs, so that your petitioner was literally chained down
neck and heels together. He was then dragged away and thrown into a
cold, damp, dark dungeon or cell, where he remained till the next day,
when he was led down before the visiting magistrates and another gentleman, who after lecturing your petitioner, and scoffing at his humiliating
and degraded situation of being so chained and ironed, they ordered your
petitioner back again into the solitary cell, where he remained in the whole
for the space of nine days and nights in this deplorable state, without being
able to put his hands to his mouth, to stand upright or lie straight, unless
it was when the chain and handcuffs were taken off for about an hour every
night, to allow your petitioner to take his bread and water and ease the calls
of nature; for the remaining 23 hours he continued in this distressing and
painful situation, with the exception of having the handcuffs off once to go
to chapel, and once or twice for a few minutes when he prayed to be suffered
to go to the privy. Thus your petitioner lay for nine days and nights without
once being allowed to have his clothes off or any relief whatsoever, with his
arms swelled with the pressure of the handcuffs to such a degree, that the
iron rings thereof were almost buried in his flesh, and when the turnkey
took them off towards the latter part of this time, they were obliged to use
considerable force and violence to get them out of the flesh! This only
excited the merriment of Pike, the turnkey, who laughed at your petitioner's
sufferings.

Your petitioner, therefore, most humbly prays your Honourable House
to take his case into your consideration, and if not afford him any relief
for his past sufferings, he most earnestly implores your Honourable House
to take such measures as will protect him and his fellow-prisoners from
such cruel and inhuman treatment in future: and your petitioner will, as
in duty bound, ever pray,

The X mark of JAMES HILLIER.

**A**  The petition of James Hillier, 1821

# 5 The new police

In 1829 Home Secretary Robert Peel set up the Metropolitan Police Force. Around 3 000 men were recruited into the new police force. They had to be under 35 years of age, in good health and they had to be able to read and write. The new policemen wore a uniform which was designed to make them look as much like civilians as possible (**A**).

The new police were not popular at first as the evidence below suggests (**B** and **C**). People called them insulting names like 'blue devils' and 'Peel's bloody gang'. The police were often harshly satirized (**D**).

By the 1830s public opinion had begun to change. People began to accept that the police force was a way of keeping law and order in London, even though there were still complaints about police brutality from time to time.

**A**  A 'Peeler' (new policeman), 1830

❛Liberty or Death! Britons and honest men! The time has at last arrived. All London meets on Tuesday. We assure you that 6 000 cutlasses have been removed from the Tower for the use of Peel's Bloody Gang. These damned police are now to be armed. Englishmen, will you put up with this?❜  (**B**)

(From a broadsheet published in 1830)

❛He will be polite and attentive to all persons of every rank and class. Insolence and rudeness will not be passed over. He must be

**D** Cartoon from 1833, attacking the 'new police'

*cautious not to interfere idly; he will act with decision and boldness. He must have a perfect command of temper, never allowing himself to be moved in the slightest degree by any language or threats. If he does his duty in a quiet and determined manner, such conduct will encourage the public to assist him should he require it.*

*Police constables are asked not to pay attention to any ignorant or silly expressions which may be made use of towards them personally. If a cab-driver is spoken to by the police, he is to be called 'cabdriver' and the vulgar word 'cabby' is never to be used.* **(C)**

(General instructions to the new police, 1829)

# Questions

**1** Describe the police uniform in **A**. Why do you think the new police wore a uniform which made them look like civilians?

**2 a** According to sources **A** to **D**, why was there a great deal of public hostility to the new police?
**b** Why do you think the 'general instructions to the new police' (**C**) were issued?
**c** In what ways does the evidence in **C** contradict the evidence in **B** and **D**?
**d** If you had been a policeman in 1837, what would you have thought of **B** and **D**?

**3 a** Which of the sources are biased against the police? How can you tell?
**b** Which sources are primary sources and why?

**4** How do most members of the public regard the police force today? How have attitudes to the police changed since 1840?

# 6 Murder!

Nineteenth century 'broadsheets' were notices which described murders, trials and executions. They were sold for about half a penny. **A** is a broadsheet about the death of John Lane and **B** is adapted from one concerning a trial for assault.

## Questions

**1** Look at **A**.
   **a** How old was John Lane when he died?
   **b** In which parish did he live?
   **c** How was he murdered?

**2 a** 'The investigation lasted eight hours.' Write down what you think John Ball might have said to the court in April 1830.
   **b** John's father is reported to have said 'I hope to God he will (die)!' Did Farmer Lane really hope his son would die?
   **c** In what way does **A** show bias against Farmer Lane?

**3** Today there are often reports of child abuse in the newspapers and on television. Why do you think some parents mistreat their children? What could be done to prevent this from happening?

**4** Look at **B**.
   **a** How old were David Gulliford and Benjamin Bartlett at the time of their execution?
   **b** What offence had they committed?
   **c** Why did they have a grudge against Hannah Richards and John Hostler?
   **d** How had Elizabeth Chinnings become involved in the case?
   **e** Summarise the court case described in **B** in your own words.

**5 a** Why do you think no evidence was 'called on behalf of the prisoners'?
   **b** Explain why Hannah Richards was 'afterwards sent to prison'.
   **c** In what way does John Hostler's evidence seem to contradict Hannah Richards'?

# A TRUE AND CORRECT ACCOUNT
## OF THE
# HORRID AND BARBAROUS
# MURDER,

*Which was committed at Buckland Saint Mary, (near Chard) on Saturday last, April 24th, 1830,*

ON THE BODY OF

# JOHN LANE,

## BY JAMES LANE, HIS FATHER.

On Monday last, an inquest was held before Mr. Caines and a respectable Jury, at the Castle Inn, Neroche Hill, on the body of JOHN LANE, aged 12.

It appeared, from many witnesses, that for a long period past, the father of the deceased, who is a small farmer, living at Deadman's Post, in the parish of Buckland Saint Mary, near Chard, had treated him with extraordinary brutality, such as beating him with a rope; at other times with a large stick; and occasionally kicking him. His treatment of the deceased was such, that the poor child was often induced to go from him, and beg for sustenance and protection among the neighbours; he was very diminutive, and looked languid; but his father compelled him to work, and on Friday last, he was seen churning butter. In the afternoon of the same day, he was seen assisting his father planting potatoes. At six o'clock the same evening, the father hailed a person who was travelling over the hill, at a short distance, and on the approach of that person, whose name is John Ball, he said to him "there's a dead body there?" pointing to the hedge. On his enquiring of him who it was, he said "'tis Jack!" meaning his son. Ball went into the field, where the poor boy lay under a hedge; he knew him, and asked him to get up; he said "I can't". The inhuman father then took him, and without hesitation threw him from the bank on which he (the father) stood, into the ditch; after which, Ball got over and lifted him out of the ditch, in which there was water. The father then came over and shook his son, and said "stand up," but he could not. The ruffian then struck him a violent blow on the forehead—deceased never spoke afterwards. Two other persons came up about this time, one of them saw the blow inflicted; the other (Geo. Bryant, of Curland,) said "Farmer Lane, you have used this boy cruelly bad, and I think he'll die before the morning." Upon which, the wretch said "I hope to God he will!" Bryant said "if he does, he'll be crowned, and you'll be sent to prison."

After this there was an attempt made to put the deceased on a horse, but not finding it an easy matter to keep him on the horse's back, Ball assisted to bear him for about forty yards, when the father took him by the arm and dragged him on about ten yards more; he then took him on his back. The eyes of the boy were closed, and his legs hung down in a lifeless state. He carried him home and threw him on the floor in the most brutal manner. The deceased never uttered a word after he received the blow on the forehead, but lingered till 7 o'clock, on Saturday morning, when he expired. In the condition described, can it be supposed that the mother could behold her offspring lingering in the agonies of death without pity or making one effort to alleviate his sufferings? It is scarcely to be credited, but she bundled him into bed when he was taken from the floor, with two other children, and took no more notice of him than if he had been a dead dog, until within an hour of his death. After hearing the evidence of the surgeons, the jury returned a verdict of Wilful Murder against James Lane, and he was committed to Ilchester goal to take his trial. The investigation lasted eight hours.

**A** The case of John Lane

**6** Look at **A** and **B**. How reliable are the sources as pieces of historical evidence? You could mention: the judge's and doctors' advice to the juries; bias against the accused; methods of recording spoken evidence; why these broadsheets were printed; who would have read the broadsheets; the lack of evidence from those accused; how the accused would have been treated in a modern court of law; other sources available to an historian.

**The life, trial, conviction and execution of David Gulliford and Benjamin Bartlett, for assaulting Hannah Richards at Shepton. Tried at Taunton and executed this day (May 2) at Ilchester.**

*David Gulliford, aged 31, and Benjamin Bartlett, aged 22, were this day executed for assaulting Hannah Richards, putting her in bodily fear and taking from her person a pelisse* (a long cloak).

Hannah Richards: *'I am 19 years of age. On the evening of the 24 March last, about 11 am, I was going down the street in Shepton, along with John Hostler, when we saw four persons standing in the market, among whom were the prisoners. As Hostler and I had given evidence at the last sessions against a brother of Bartlett's, we turned out of the way to avoid meeting them, knowing they had a spite against us. As we were going down a back lane, they overtook us, and one of them dragged me across a wall into the field. Then the four set about dragging me along the field into a shrubbery. From that they dragged me back again, and the prisoners put me into a pond up to the breast. Having kept me there awhile, they took me out, laid me on my back and took off my pelisse. One of them took 9s 5d* (47p) *out of my pocket saying that they should keep it, as it was James Bartlett's money, meaning the person who had been convicted at the sessions on my evidence. Having done all this, they pulled up my clothes around my head and left me lying there. I got up as soon as I could and went to Elizabeth Chinnings' house. I knocked at the door and asked her to let me in. The four men followed me, and were throwing stones and dirt at me while I was at the door. Elizabeth Chinnings put her head out of the window and said as I had so many men after me she would not let me in. I then went to the churchyard and laid down. Shortly after, John Hostler came up and took me home. Next morning I found my pelisse in a corner of the field, covered in dirt and stones. I was scratched and bruised all over. I was afterwards sent to prison by the magistrate lest I should make it up with them, as they wanted me to do. I was crying murder all along while they were abusing me.'*

John Hostler: *'When the four men came to us, one of them dragged her across a wall. I believe they did not see me. I hid myself because I was afraid of them as they had threatened me before, on account of the evidence I gave at the sessions. Gulliford had offered 5s* (25p) *to Hannah Richards to buy something to poison me.'*

Elizabeth Chinnings supported that part of the evidence of Hannah Richards which related to her.

Joseph Parsons, a constable, saw Hannah Richards on the following morning. She was then bleeding all over and very weak. Her skin was off her arms in several places.

No evidence having been called on behalf of the prisoners, the jury found them guilty. Mr Justice Park looked upon the conduct of the prisoners as outrageous. He could not prevent the extreme penalty of the law from being carried out in this case. His Lordship, after a suitable address, sentenced the prisoners to be hanged.'

**B** The case of David Gulliford and Benjamin Bartlett

# 7 Prison life

Sources **A–C** provide us with information about prison life in Somerset in 1850.

Look through the documents carefully. Then answer the questions below.

## Questions

**1** Define the following words with the help of a dictionary: oakum (**A**); gruel (**B**); tepid (**C**); fermented (**C**); capstan (**A**); flax (**A**).

**2 a** According to **A**, how did 'relaxation' during the first three months of conviction differ from relaxation during the remainder of a prisoner's sentence?

**b** What was the difference between a class 1 prisoner and a class 2 prisoner (**A** and **B**)?

**c** Do you think the rules in **C** were harsh? Why do you think they were imposed?

**d** Do prisoners today have to accept rules as harsh as these?

**3** Look at **B**.

**a** What source of nutrition seems to be missing from the prisoners' diet?

**b** How might the poor diet have affected prisoners' work and behaviour?

**c** Which group of prisoners were given extra food? How do you explain this?

**4** In the 1820s, Robert Peel and Elizabeth Fry had argued in favour of a prison system that tried to reform rather than punish convicted criminals. However, documents **A–C** reveal a harsh, punitive prison system in 1850. How do you explain this? You could mention: changes in public opinion; changes in government; increased crime-rate; costs; an increasing prison population; the deaths of Peel (1850) and Elizabeth Fry (1845).

## 81. — Classification and Labor Table for Convicted Prisoners —

Hard Labor of 1st Class to consist of Tread Wheel, Crank, Shaft, Pump, Capstan, Stonebreaking, Flax Beating by Twinge, and Flax Breaking by Crank or Rope Beating, Oakum Picking as supplementary to non-effective Labor.

Hard Labor of 2nd Class to consist of Oakum or Rope Picking, Picking, Decorating, Mat-Making, Weaving.

Employment for Criminal Prisoners not sentenced to Hard Labor to consist of Oakum Picking, Mat-Making, or other Industrial Labor —

28 & 29 Vic. ch. 126 s. 19, 21. Scot: Aug: 45, 46, 47, 38.

| Time | Class | Hard Labor, 1st Class | Hard Labor, 2nd Class | Employment | Promotion | Relaxation | Restriction |
|---|---|---|---|---|---|---|---|
| First Three Months | 1 | 8 hours Tread Wheel, Crank or Stonebreaking and 2 hours Oakum Picking | 10 hours Oakum Picking | 10 hours Oakum Picking, 2 hours in the open air — | 1 good Mark required every day to raise to Class 2 — | Bible and Prayer Book, no secular Book, no Work — | Keep on Plank Bed, no Mattress |
| Remainder of Sentence | 2 | 4 hours Tread Wheel, Crank or Stonebreaking, and 6 hours other labor — | 4 hours Oakum Picking, and 6 hours other labor | 10 hours Industrial Labor or other employment — | — | Slate and secular Books and may write and receive one letter every 3 months, one hour's exercise if at work in Cell. | — |

Rules adjusting Marks

Promotion from 1st Class to 2nd Class to be dependent on industry and good conduct — Prisoner may be degraded to Class 1 for misconduct — The Medical Officer to determine the description of hard labor a Prisoner is competent to perform — Prisoner for hard labor for 14 days at least, to do 10 hours Oakum Picking, and not to leave their Cells except to go to Chapel — Female Prisoners sentenced to hard labor to pick not less than 3 lbs of Oakum a day, unless their labor be required in the services of the Prison — Prisoner in Class 2 may receive education out of hours appointed for other labor —

Industrial Prisoner whose conduct is good to receive one good mark daily, thus — (/) —
Prisoner careless or not sufficiently diligent to receive one indifferent mark, thus — (○) —
Idle or badly conducted Prisoner to receive one bad mark thus — (\) —
N.B. One different marks leave Prisoner stationary — One bad mark cancels one good one —
At Oakum, issued to Prisoners will be weighed when Picked — Prisoner may be allowed to see their respective Mark Register and may appeal thereon to the Governor or Deputy Governor —

A  Classification and labour table

* Scotch American Scale? Bad may to turn on the judgment of the Rocks, Hops, and Peas.

26, 29, Vic. c. 126, Sec. 31.

# 75. THE DIETARY FOR PRISONERS.

Male prisoners at Hard Labour, at Treadwheel, Crank, Flax and Rope Beating, and women employed in the laundry or other laborious occupation, to have the following additions and substitutions.

In Class 2—1 ounce extra of cheese on Sundays, and one pint of gruel for supper daily.

In classes 2, 3, 4, and 5, —1 ounce extra of cheese on Sundays.

In lieu of the pudding on Mondays and Fridays,—3 ounces of beef in class 3; 4 ounces in Class 4; and 4 ounces in Class 5 for men; and 2 ounces in Class 3; 3 ounces in Class 4; and 3 ounces in Class 5, for women.

The meat to be weighed after cooking, and served cold.

The meat liquor on Mondays and Fridays to form part of the soup on Tuesdays and Saturdays.

The soup to contain in each pint 2 ounces of split peas, instead of 1 ounce of barley.

| Meals. | Days of the Week. | Articles of Food. | CLASS 1 One week or less. | | CLASS 2 After 1 Week and up to the 1st Month inclusive. | | CLASS 3 After 1 Month and up to the 3rd Month, inclusive. | | CLASS 4 After 3 Months and up to the 6th Month, inclusive. | | CLASS 5 After 6 Months. | |
|---|---|---|---|---|---|---|---|---|---|---|---|---|
| | | | Men. | Women. | Men. | Women. | Men. | Women. | Men. | Women. | Men. | Women. |
| | | | Ounces | Ounces | Ounces | Ounces | Ounces | Ounces | Ounces | Ounces | Ounces | Ounces |
| Breakfast | Every day | Bread | 6 | 5 | 6 | 5 | 8 | 6 | 8 | 6 | 8 | 6 |
| | | Gruel | .. | .. | 1 pint | 1 pint | 1 pint | 1 pint | 1 pint* | 1 pint* | 1 pint* | 1 pint* |
| Supper | Every day | Bread | 6 | 5 | 6 | 5 | 6 | 6 | 8 | 6 | 8 | 6 |
| | | Gruel | .. | .. | 1 pint | 1 pint | 1 pint | 1 pint | 1 pint | 1 pint | 1 pint* | 1 pint* |
| | Sunday | Bread | 8 | 6 | 8 | 6 | 10 | 8 | 10 | 8 | 12 | 10 |
| | | Cheese | .. | .. | 1 | 1 | 2 | 2 | 2 | 2 | 3 | 2 |
| | Monday, Wednesday and Friday | Bread | 6 | 5 | 6 | 5 | 4 | 4 | 4 | 4 | 4 | 4 |
| | | Potatoes | .. | .. | .. | .. | 12 | 8 | 16 | 12 | 16 | 12 |
| Dinner | | Suet Pudding | .. | .. | .. | .. | 8 | 6 | 12 | 8 | 12 | 8 |
| | Wednesday and Friday | Indian-meal Pudding | 6 | 4 | 8 | 6 | .. | .. | .. | .. | .. | .. |
| | Tuesday, Thursday and Saturday | Bread | 6 | 5 | 6 | 5 | 8 | 6 | 8 | 6 | 8 | 8 |
| | | Potatoes | 8 | 6 | 12 | 8 | 8 | 6 | 8 | 6 | 16 | 12 |
| | | Soup | .. | .. | .. | .. | 1 pint | 1 pint | 1 pint | 1 pint | 1 pint | 1 pint |

### Ingredients of Soup.

In every pint:
The meat and liquor from 6 ounces of the necks, legs, and shins of beef, weighed with the bone, previous to cooking.
1 ounce of onions or leeks.
1 ounce of Scotch barley.
2 ounces of carrots, parsnips, turnips, or other cheap vegetable, with pepper and salt.
On Tuesdays and Saturdays, the meat liquor of the previous day is to be added.

### Ingredients of Suet Pudding.

1¼ ounces of suet.
6¼ ounces of flour, and about 8 ounces of water to make 1 pound.

### Ingredients of Indian-meal Pudding.

To consist of half-a-pint of skimmed milk, to every 6 ounces of meal.

### Ingredients of Gruel.

To every pint, 2 ounces of coarse Scotch oatmeal, with salt.
* The Gruel for breakfast on Sunday in Class 4, and for breakfast and supper in Class 5, to contain 1 ounce of molasses.

Prisoners for examination, before trial, misdemeanants of the first division who do not maintain themselves, and destitute debtors, the diet of Class 3 without Hard Labour, for any period not exceeding one calendar month; that of Class 4, after the expiration of one month, and till the completion of the second calendar month; and that of Class 5 if the detention should exceed two calendar months.

Debtors or bankrupts committed by County Courts, or by any Court of Law for fraud, and deserters on route, the diet of Class 3.

Prisoners under punishment for prison offences under the provisions of the 42nd Section of the Prison Act, to have the Diet of Class 4 for the first seven days; and after that to have 2 ounces extra of bread per diem.

Prisoners may be placed in a lower Class of the Dietary by order of a Visiting Justice, with the sanction of the Medical Officer.

B  Dietary table for prisoners

## 26

### ABSTRACT OF REGULATIONS AND RULES

for the Government of the Prisons at Taunton and Shepton Mallet, as directed by Prisons' Act, 28 and 29, Vic. c. 126, Sch. 1, Reg. 72.

1. Every prisoner shall be searched on admission, and all articles taken from him; but no prisoner shall be searched in the presence of another prisoner. All money and other effects belonging to prisoners shall be taken charge of by the Governor, and a record kept of them.

2. An exact description of every criminal prisoner shall be recorded in a register at the time of his admission. He shall then be placed in a reception cell, and shall not be passed into his proper class until he has been examined by the surgeon and cleansed in a tepid bath.

3. Every convicted criminal prisoner shall wear the prison dress.

4. Every male prisoner shall sleep in a cell by himself, or under special circumstances in a separate bed in a cell with not less than two other male prisoners. Bed clothes shall be provided for every prisoner. A convicted criminal prisoner shall sleep on a plank bed without mattress, in accordance with the rules of the prison.

5. Bed clothes shall be aired every day, and sheets washed once a month. Sheets used by one prisoner shall not be transferred to another until they have been washed.

*Margin notes (left column):*

General Rules.

1. Prisoners on entrance to be searched.
28, 29, Vic. c. 126, Sch. 1, Reg. 6, 7, 8.

2. Descriptive Register.
28, 29, Vic. c. 126, Sch. 1, Reg. 9.

3. Dress of convicted Criminals.
28, 29, Vic. c. 126, Sch. 1, Reg. 23.

4. Beds.
28, 29, Vic. c. 126, Sch. 1, Reg. 28, and Labor Table, Prison Rules.

5. Bed Clothes.
28, 29, Vic. c. 126, Sch. 1, Reg. 27, Prison Rules 12, 13.

## 27

6. Every prisoner shall wash his hands and face once a day, and his feet once a week, and, unless exempted by the surgeon, have a tepid bath once a month.

No prisoner's hair shall be cut closer than is necessary for health and cleanliness; but every prisoner not wearing his beard shall be shaved on admission, and not less than once a week. Female prisoners' hair shall not be cut without their consent, except when necessary on account of vermin or dirt.

7. No criminal prisoner shall upon any pretence, speak to, or by any sign, writing, or otherwise, hold any communication with another prisoner. Every criminal prisoner on leaving his cell shall keep such distance from every other prisoner as shall be directed by the officer in charge.

8. Every convicted criminal prisoner shall be subsisted on the dietary established for the prison. All provisions supplied to prisoners shall be of proper quality and weight. Scales and legal weights and measures shall be provided open to the use of any prisoner under restrictions made by the prison rules.

9. No convicted criminal prisoner shall be allowed any wine, beer, or other fermented liquor, without an order in writing from the surgeon, or shall receive any food, clothing, bedding, or necessaries other than the prison allowance, except by special order of one or more visiting justices.

10. No convicted criminal prisoner, or prisoner for examination or trial, shall be allowed the use of tobacco.

*Margin notes (right column):*

General Rules.

6. Personal cleanliness.
29, 29, Vic. c. 126, Sch. 1, Reg. 28, 29.
Prison Rules 9, 10, 11.

7. Prisoners not to hold communication.
Prison Rule 81.

8. Dietary.
28, 29, Vic. c. 126, Sch. 1, Reg. 21.
Prison Rule 14.

9. No Wine or Beer, except by order of Surgeon.
28, 29, Vic. c. 126, Sch. 1, Reg. 23.

10. No Tobacco.
Prison Rule 87.

C  Regulations and rules

# 8 Wanted!

## £1 REWARD.

Whereas a thief or thieves have lately at different times stolen from the front of the Dwelling House of Mr. DOMMETT several

# CHRYSANTHEMUMS

AND A

## ROSE TREE,

the above reward will be paid on conviction of the offender or offenders to any person giving such information as will lead to detection.

Dated January 20th, 1861   T. YOUNG, PRINTER, &c., FORE STREET, CHARD.

**A**

## £5 REWARD.

WHEREAS some Person or Persons, during the Night of June 1st, did Wilfully Destroy, by means of Lime, a quantity of FISH in the RIVER, near DONIFORD, in the Parish of St. Decuman's,

The above Reward will be paid to any Person, on whose evidence the Offender or Offenders shall be convicted.

A. V. HORNE,
STEWARD.

*Orchard Wyndham, 2nd June, 1893.*

COX BROTHERS, PRINTERS, "FREE PRESS" OFFICE, WILLITON.

**B**

# CANNINGTON ASSOCIATION,

FOR THE

*Preventing of Depredations,*

AND FOR THE BETTER, MORE SPEEDY AND EFFECTUAL

DETECTING, APPREHENDING, AND

# PROSECUTING

## OF PERSONS COMMITTING OFFENCES

Against the Persons and Property of the Members of such Association,
and of the Aiders, Abettors, and Accessaries of such Offenders.

AT a General Meeting of the Subscribers of this Parish, assembled on
the 9th day of March, 1831, it was Resolved that it be Advertised
that the following

# REWARDS

Will be Paid by the Secretary, for the time being, to any Person or
Persons who shall give such Information to him, as may lead to the
Conviction of any Person or Persons who shall be guilty of the follow-
ing Offences against the Persons or Properties of the Members of the
Association, that is to say:

| | £ | s. | d. |
|---|---|---|---|
| Of burglary; house-breaking; highway robbery; stealing from the person; assaulting with an intent to rob; setting fire to any house, barn or out-house; or to any mow or stack of corn, grain, straw, hay, or wood; breaking into any barn, or out-house; maliciously killing or maiming or wounding any horse or sheep; stealing any horse or sheep; or of being accessary to, or being concerned in aiding or abetting any of the said offences, the sum of...... | 10 | 0 | 0 |
| Of stealing, maiming, or maliciously wounding any other cattle, or any pig; of stealing poultry of any sort, or any hay, straw, seed, corn, or grain, thrashed or unthrashed; of buying or receiving stolen goods, knowing the same to be stolen; or of any other capital offence than aforesaid; or of being accessary to any of these offences, or to any capital offence, the sum of...... | 5 | 0 | 0 |
| Of stealing any instrument of husbandry or trade; of cutting, lopping, or damaging any tree; of stealing wood or underwood, or apples or fruit of any denomination; of breaking, or damaging, or steal-ing, any bridge in any footpath, or any hedge, gate, hurdle, bar, pale, rail, post, hooks or eyes of gates, locks, or other iron work, or lead from any dwelling-house; robbing any garden, orchard or nurs-ery ground; stealing or destroying turnips, roots, or other vegetables in any field, enclosed ground or other place, if amounting to felony | 1 | 0 | 0 |
| And in any of the cases last mentioned, not amounting to felony, and for the committing of any other wilful or malicious injury or tres-pass, punishable in a summary way before Magistrates, the sum of | | 10 | 0 |

And the Secretary, if he see occasion, is to cause Handbills to be
distributed and pursuit to be made after any Person or Persons suspected of any Crime for the discovery of which a Reward is offered by
this Society; and offer the Reward abovementioned in regard to the
particular Offence, by Advertisements in the public Papers and otherwise, for the discovery of any such Person or Persons.

LIST OF SUBSCRIBERS.

| | | | |
|---|---|---|---|
| LORD CLIFFORD. | A. BLAKE, ESQ. | MR. LEIGH. | MR. CAVILL. |
| HON. P. P. BOUVERIE. | J. LINDON, ESQ. | MR. HEMBRY. | MR. SHEPHERD. |
| MISS TAYLOR. | MR. MURRAY. | MR. HOBBS. | MR. ALLEN. |
| REV. R. DAVIS. | MR. TUCKER. | MR. BURNELL. | MR. R. TAYLOR |
| C. KNIGHT, ESQ. | MR. MERRYMAN. | MR. G. SILK. | MR. H. MAY. |
| J. KNIGHT, ESQ. | MR. MORLE. | MR. H. COLES. | MR. W. NORTH. |

## ARTHUR BLAKE, Secretary.

Geo. Awbrey, Printer, Fore Street, Bridgwater.

C

# Questions

**1 a** What seems strange about **A**?

**b** What motive would a person have had for destroying 'by means
of lime a quantity of fish' (**B**)?

**c** According to **C**, how much reward could you have claimed if you
had informed on a person (**i**) scrumping apples (**ii**) committing arson
(**iii**) receiving stolen goods?

# SHEEP STEALING.

**WHEREAS** on the night of Tuesday, the **27th** day of June last, a HORN EWE SHEEP was stolen from the Fold of *Mr. John Major House*, at *Chard Farm*, Chard, Somerset.

WE, THE UNDERSIGNED DO HEREBY OFFER

# £50 REWARD

to any person or persons who will give such information as will lead to the discovery and Conviction of the Offender or Offenders, to be paid on Conviction.

N.B. If two or more persons were concerned, and either will impeach and give information against the other, the person so impeaching, shall on Conviction, be entitled to the above Reward.

| | £. | s. | d. | | £. | s. | d. |
|---|---|---|---|---|---|---|---|
| The Right Hon. EARL POULETT | 5 | 0 | 0 | JOHN WALL | 2 | 0 | 0 |
| W. LOVERIDGE, Esq. | 2 | 0 | 0 | SIMEON SCOTT | 2 | 0 | 0 |
| THOMAS DEANE, Esq. | 2 | 0 | 0 | BENJN. BEVISS | 2 | 0 | 0 |
| Messrs. SALTER & CLARKE | 2 | 0 | 0 | JON. HECKS | 2 | 0 | 0 |
| NATHANIEL JEFFERY | 1 | 0 | 0 | JOHN HECKS | 2 | 0 | 0 |
| FREDERICK BOND | 2 | 0 | 0 | JAMES HULL | 2 | 0 | 0 |
| JOHN WALE | 2 | 0 | 0 | W. DEANE | 2 | 0 | 0 |
| WM. NOTLEY | 2 | 0 | 0 | THOS. DAVIS HILLARD | 2 | 0 | 0 |
| WM. HOUSE | 2 | 0 | 0 | JAMES G. SHEPPARD | 2 | 0 | 0 |
| WM. BENTLEY | 2 | 0 | 0 | WM. DEANE | 2 | 0 | 0 |
| JOHN DEANE | 2 | 0 | 0 | WM. READ | 2 | 0 | 0 |
| JOHN M. HOUSE | 2 | 0 | 0 | GEORGE ENGLAND | 2 | 0 | 0 |

Dated Chard, July 7th, 1854.—NOWLEN, PRINTER, " GENERAL ADVERTISER OFFICE," CHARD.

**D**

**d** According to **D**, how was the money for the reward going to be raised? Why do you think the ewe was considered to be so valuable?

**2 a** What do you notice about the sizes of the rewards in relation to the offences committed?
**b** How many sources contain references to: (**i**) vandalism; (**ii**) theft; (**iii**) violence against the person?
**c** Who would have decided to have had the notices printed? Why didn't they simply put the matter in the hands of the police?

**3** Using details from these notices and other sources write a full report about attitudes to crime and punishment between 1850 and 1900.

# Section V
# TRADE UNIONS

# 1 Rawfolds Mill

In 1812 there was a serious economic depression. Food prices were high and in many parts of the country there was mass unemployment. In the textile areas of Yorkshire, groups of workers put pressure on their employers to increase wages and improve working conditions. There were threats to smash up textile machines and burn down mills. The workers claimed that their leader was 'General Ned Ludd', a textile worker who lived in Sherwood Forest. In fact, there was no such person as Ned Ludd although we still call machine-breakers Luddites. **A** is from a television programme about the Luddites.

**A** 'Luddites' from a Thames Television programme

Sources **D–H** describe a Luddite attack on a textile mill in the West Riding of Yorkshire (**B**). The owner of the mill was William Cartwright. Source **C** explains why Cartwright's mill was a Luddite target. As you are reading through the sources consider how reliable each of them is.

RAWFOLDS MILL.

**B**  Rawfolds Mill, Yorkshire

❝ *Mr Cartwright had dared to use machinery for the cropping of woollen cloth, which was an unpopular measure in 1812, when many other circumstances conspired to make the condition of mill-hands unbearable from the pressure of starvation and misery.* ❞  (**C**)

(From *The Letters of Mrs Gaskell*, 1845)

❝ *At Rawfolds, near Cleckheaton, a gentleman of the·name of William Cartwright has a mill used for the purpose of dressing cloth in the way objected to by the men. On Saturday night, about 12.30 am, a number of armed men surprised the two sentries outside the mill, and having secured their arms and persons, made a violent attack upon the mill, broke in the window frames and fired a volley of shots into the premises. The guards inside the mill grabbed their weapons and fired upon their attackers; this fire was returned and repeated during the battle, the mob all the time trying to force their way in, but without success, a number of voices crying 'Bang up,' 'Murder them!', 'Pull down the door!' For about 20 minutes the battle continued, till at length the firing and hammering died down, and soon after the whole body of men retreated, leaving such of their men as could not join in the retreat. During the battle 140 shots were fired from the mill. The alarm bell in the mill was rung and a large number of stones were thrown from the roof, which had an instant effect,* otherwise a quantity of oil and vitriol (acid) would have been poured down. When the firing had stopped, the guards heard the cries of two unfortunate men, lying in their own blood, and writhing under the torture of terrible wounds. 'For God's sake' cried one, 'shoot me – put me out of my misery!' 'Oh!' cried the other, 'Help, help! I know all and I will tell all!' On the arrival of more soldiers, these men were carried to the Star Inn and medical aid was called in. One of them turned out to be a cropper of the name of Samuel Hartley. The other was John Booth, about 19 years of age, son of a clergyman in Craven. Hartley had received a shot in his chest which had passed through his body and lodged beneath the skin at the left shoulder, from whence it was extracted with a portion of bone. He died at three o'clock on Monday morning. Booth's wound was in his leg which was shattered almost to atoms; he had to have his leg ampu-tated but owing to the extreme loss of blood before the surgeon arrived, spasms came on during the operation and he died at six o'clock on Sunday morning. **)** (D)

(*Leeds Mercury*, 14 April 1812)

**(** *There was a crash – smash – shiver. A volley of stones struck the front of the mill. Now every pane of glass lay shattered. A yell followed – a rioters' yell – a North of England – a Yorkshire " a West-Riding yell.*

Shots were fired by the rioters. Had the defenders waited for this signal? It seemed so. The mill awoke: fire flashed from its empty window-frames; a volley of gunfire rang through the Hollow. What was going on now? It was difficult to see in the darkness, but something terrible was going on; fierce attacks and counter-attacks; the mill yard, the mill itself, was full of battle movement; there was firing all the time; there was struggling, rushing, trampling and shouting between. The aim of the attackers seemed to be to enter the mill, that of the defendants to beat them off. They heard the rebel leader shout 'To the back, lads!' They heard a voice reply, 'Come round, we will meet you!'

Moore had expected this attack for days, perhaps weeks: he was prepared for it at every point. He had fortified and defended his mill, which in itself was a strong building: he was a cool, brave man who was willing to stand his ground. The rioters had never been so met before. At other mills they had attacked, they had found no resistance. When their leaders saw the steady fire being kept up from the mill, they felt that nothing was to be done here. In haste, they regrouped their forces, drew them away from the building: a roll was called *over, in which the men answered to figures instead of names: they scattered wide over the fields, leaving silence and ruin behind them. The attack had lasted barely an hour.* **(E)**

(From *Shirley* by Charlotte Brontë, 1849)

6 *The attack on Rawfolds has become famous. Perhaps 150 Luddites took part. Led by George Mellor, a young cropper from Longroyd Bridge near Huddersfield, the Luddites exchanged a brisk fire with the defenders for 20 minutes. Under cover of this fire, a small party of hammermen and men with hatchets made repeated attempts to break down the heavy doors of the mill. This party suffered serious casualties, at least five being wounded, two of whom were left behind when the Luddites suddenly retreated. It is said that Mellor was the last to leave the field, and that he could not help the two wounded men since he was helping to carry another (his own cousin) to safety. The ground around the mill was littered with muskets, axes, pikes and metal implements. A thousand details of this attack entered into the folklore both of the masters and the populace. At this point we should pause to enquire why . . .One part of the background is given in Charlotte Brontë's 'Shirley'. The mill-owner, Gerard Moore (modelled on Cartwright) is rightly shown as belonging to the half-Whig, half-Radical, middle class whose organ was the 'Leeds Mercury' . . . 'Shirley's' limitations, of course, are in the treatment of the Luddites and their sympathisers. But the novel remains a true expression of the middle-class myth.* **(F)**

(E P Thompson, *The Making of the English Working Class*, 1963)

6 *William Cartwright had a mill near Liversedge which was attacked one night by about 200 men armed with guns, pistols, stakes and hammers. He had several soldiers with him to ward off the attack. Cartwright wrote 'The attackers being driven back we found they had left behind them two men mortally wounded, who despite their grievous condition refused to talk about their associates.' The two men were Booth, a lad of 19, and Hartley, a former worker at Cartwright's mill, aged 24. They lay bleeding in the courtyard of the mill and Cartwright forbade anyone to touch them until they gave him the names of the leaders. In the morning when a crowd gathered, Cartwright was obliged to allow someone to carry them into a house and summon a doctor. A clergyman went with them and urged the suffering men to tell him the names of the leaders. At last Booth raised his head. 'Can you keep a secret?' he asked; 'I can,' replied the clergyman. 'So can I!' answered Booth, who soon after died. Hartley died the following morning.* **(G)**

(A M Newth, *Britain and the World 1789–1901*, 1967)

❝Breaking through the gates, the Luddites hurled themselves upon the mill, a large, four-storey building, with rows of windows fronting a yard. Hammers battered on the door but with no result, for it was so studded with nails that the blows made no impression. Meanwhile the defenders began firing down from the safety of the first floor, and the mill bell clanged out to summon reinforcements.

Under constant fire, the Luddites fought to get into the mill, hacking at doors and windows, attempting to swarm up the walls. Mellor tried a second line of attack round the back but there was only a narrow strip of ground between the building and the mill dam and one man fell into the water. The defenders fired down until many Luddites were wounded. Mellor saw that it was hopeless. He ordered his men to scatter taking the wounded who could walk, but two could not be moved – Samuel Hartley, a Halifax cropper, and John Booth, a clergyman's son. Mellor fled last of all with 'tears of rage and pity in his eyes.'

Cartwright came out of the mill, and many other people appeared, awoken by the noise. One was Hammond Roberson, a clergyman, characterised by Charlotte Brontë in 'Shirley' as Mr Helstone. They found all the mill windows broken, the yard covered with wreckage and weapons, and the two Luddites groaning in agony. The two young men were carried to a nearby inn where a doctor decided that Booth's leg would have to be amputated. He was too weak from loss of blood to stand the shock of the operation and it was obvious to all that he was dying.

He signalled to the clergyman, who was hovering in the room, hoping to hear a last confession. Booth gasped 'Can you keep a secret?'
'I can!', Roberson answered eagerly.
'So can I!' murmured Booth; and with his secret intact, he died. Samuel Hartley died two days later.❞ **(H)**

(Angela Bull, *The Machine Breakers*, 1980)

# Questions

**1 a** Make notes on the main events described in each of the sources.
**b** What differences and similarities do you notice in the way the sources describe the attack on the mill? How do you explain these differences and similarities?
**c** Write your own version of what you think happened and why at Rawfolds Mill in April 1812.

# 2 The Tolpuddle Martyrs

Early on 24 February 1834, George Loveless and five other Dorset farm workers were arrested by local constable James Brine. The farm workers were charged with swearing a secret illegal oath and sent to Dorchester Gaol. Later, George Loveless described what happened (**A**).

> ❛On 15 March we were taken to the County-hall to await our trial. . . As to the trial I need mention but little; the whole proceedings showed a shameful disregard for justice and decency; the grand jury appeared to ransack heaven and earth to get some clue against us but in vain; our characters were investigated from our childhood to the present moment; our masters were asked if we were idle or attended public houses or some other fault in us. When nothing whatever could be raked together, the unjust and cruel judge, John Williams, ordered us to be tried for mutiny and conspiracy under an Act 37 Geo. III for the suppression of mutiny amongst the marines and seamen, several years ago at the Nore. The greater part of the evidence against us, on our trial, was put into the mouths of the witnesses by the judge; and when he evidently wished them to say any particular thing, and the witness would say 'I cannot remember,' he would say 'Now think: I will give you another minute to consider.' He would then repeat over the words and ask 'Cannot you remember?' Sometimes they would merely answer 'Yes' and the judge would set the words down as proceeding from the witness. I shall not forget his words when summing up the evidence, among other things he told the jury that if trade societies were allowed to exist, it would ruin masters, cause a stagnation in trade, destroy property.❜  (**A**)

The farm workers were found guilty. The judge gave each of the men the maximum sentence – seven years transportation to Australia.

The 'Tolpuddle Martyrs' were all transported to Australia. But there was such an outcry against their sentences that two years later, in 1836, the government pardoned the six men.

Unfortunately no official transcript of the trial mentioned in **A** was ever produced. The dialogue below is based on newspaper reports of March 1834. There was wide coverage of the trial and the reports in various papers are remarkably similar. We can therefore assume that they are fairly accurate.

**Scene** The Court House, Dorchester **Date** Monday March 17 1834

**Present at the trial:**
Mr Justice Williams – Judge
Sir John Gambier – Counsel for the Prosecution
Mr Derbishire – Counsel for the Defence
Edward Legg – Labourer
Mrs Mary Whetham – Shopkeeper

. . . . . . . . . .

| | | |
|---|---|---|
| Gambier | : | *Let me read out again the charges against the prisoners. The men in the dock are charged with forcing Edward Legg, a labourer, to take an unlawful oath in December 1833. The purpose of this oath was to force Legg not to give away the secrets of a farm workers' society. We are going to argue that forcing someone to take an oath such as this is illegal. We also intend to show that any society that forces its members to accept such an oath is illegal. I would like to call Edward Legg to the witness box. (Legg enters the witness box.) Tell the court where you live and what your job is.* |
| Legg | : | *I come from Affpuddle. I'm a farm labourer.* |
| Gambier | : | *Will you tell the court what happened to you on December 9, 1833.* |
| Legg | : | *I was in my cottage that evening. There was a tap at the window. It was James Brine and James Hammett. Brine said to me 'Are you along to Tolpuddle with us, Edward?' I had heard there was some sort of meeting down there. I asked them if they would want me to swear to anything. Brine said 'We need to see how many men we can gather together. If the masters won't pay us a living wage, then we will have to make them.' Well, we went to Tolpuddle together and we met up with three other men on the way. Then we all went to Thomas Standfield's house.* |
| Gambier | : | *Were the Loveless brothers there already?* |
| Legg | : | *I think so. When we got inside, somebody said 'Put the blind-folds on Edward and John Lock.' They tied handkerchiefs over our eyes. They led us up to the upstairs room in the cottage. Someone talked about our wages. Then we had to kneel down.* |
| Gambier | : | *What exactly was said? And who said it?* |
| Legg | : | *Well, Sir, I didn't recognise the voice and I didn't know what it was all about. They just asked us to kneel down.* |
| Gambier | : | *Was anything said about striking for higher wages?* |
| Legg | : | *I'm not sure, Sir.* |
| Judge | : | *Think again. I will give you one minute.* (Pause) |
| Legg | : | *That might have been it. Something about striking for wages.* |
| Gambier | : | *Did you get the impression that they really intended to strike?* |
| Legg | : | *I suppose so. They said we could do the same if we liked.* |

| | | |
|---|---|---|
| Gambier | : | *Did they ask you to pay anything?* |
| Legg | : | *They said we would pay one shilling at first, then a penny a week afterwards.* |
| Gambier | : | *Did you have to kiss a book while you were blindfolded?* |
| Legg | : | *Yes. And before that someone read from a book. But I don't know what it was.* |
| Gambier | : | *Was it about your souls?* |
| Legg | : | *That might have been it.* |
| Judge | : | *Think carefully, Legg. This is important.* |
| Gambier | : | *Was it that your souls would be roasted in hell if you did not keep the secrets of the society?* |
| Legg | : | *Yes, I think that was it.* |
| Gambier | : | *Who read the words?* |
| | | *(Pause)* |
| Legg | : | *I think it might have been James Loveless.* |
| Gambier | : | *When the handkerchiefs were removed, what did you see?* |
| Legg | : | *I saw the six men in the dock, Sir.* |
| Gambier | : | *Were John and George Loveless wearing their usual clothes?* |
| Legg | : | *No. They had on something like a surplice or a smock.* |
| Gambier | : | *Was there a Bible on the table?* |
| Legg | : | *I saw a book. It might have been a Bible.* |
| Judge | : | *Well, was it a Bible or not?* |
| Legg | : | *Sir, I can't say. It was just a book.* |
| Gambier | : | *Was there a picture of a skeleton in the room?* |
| Legg | : | *There was a picture there. They said it was a picture of Death, Sir.* |
| Gambier | : | *Did they use the words 'Society' or 'Brothers' at all?* |
| Legg | : | *Yes, I believe they did.* |
| Gambier | : | *That is all, M'Lud.* |
| Derbishire | : | *Legg, you know the prisoners standing in the dock?* |
| Legg | : | *Yes, Sir.* |
| Derbishire | : | *What do local people think of these prisoners? Would you say they are well liked?* |
| Legg | : | *They are all respectable, hard-working men. I have never heard a word said against them.* |
| Derbishire | : | *Well then are you surprised to see them standing in the dock?* |
| Legg | : | *Yes, Sir, I can't see they've done wrong.* |
| Judge | : | *Mr Derbishire, this has very little bearing on the case.* |
| Derbishire | : | *No further questions, M'Lud.* |
| Gambier | : | *I would now like to call Mrs Mary Whetham.* |
| | | *(Mrs Whetham enters the witness box. She takes the oath.)* |
| Gambier | : | *Please tell the court who you are and what you do.* |
| Whetham | : | *My name is Mary Whetham. Me and my husband keep a paint shop in Dorchester.* |
| Gambier | : | *Will you tell the court what you know about James Loveless?* |
| Whetham | : | *Well Sir, James Loveless came to the shop sometime in October 1833. He gave me two designs he wanted painting, one of Death and one of a skeleton, six feet high on a dark background. Oh, and he wanted the words 'Remember thine end' painted over the head of Death.* |
| Gambier | : | *Did your husband paint these pictures?* |
| Whetham | : | *No, he didn't like the look of them. John saw James Loveless in the Antelope Inn later on and said he wasn't going to paint them.* |

| Gambier | : | *What did Loveless say?* |
|---|---|---|
| Whetham | : | *You must ask my husband, Sir.* |
| Gambier | : | *What happened to the designs?* |
| Whetham | : | *They were destroyed. They went into the fire. I didn't like the look of them.* |
| Gambier | : | *Could we now call Mr Whetham?* |

(Whetham supports Mrs Whetham's story. The counsel for the defence ask the Whethams a series of questions. Then Sir John Gambier sums up the case for the prosecution. Finally, Mr Derbishire makes a plea on behalf of the prisoners.)

Derbishire : *I submit to the court that two things must be proved. First, that the prisoners have administered an illegal oath; second, that they have formed an illegal association or trades union. On both counts I believe there is insufficient evidence to find the prisoners guilty.*

*As to the oath, we have the evidence of one unreliable witness who told us that at one meeting some words which he didn't understand were spoken by someone he didn't know. This is not, M'lud, sufficient evidence that an unlawful oath was administered.*

*As for the illegal association, there has been no evidence put forward connecting the prisoners in the dock with the Act of 1797. The Act was passed to deal with naval mutinies and to suppress any society formed for the purpose of disturbing the peace. In the rules of the farm labourers' society it was stated that the object of the society was to provide a fund for helping members in time of need. The prisoners are poor working men with wives and children to support. I cannot see how such a society can be considered illegal.*

(The judge sums up what has been said and advises the jury. The jury retire to discuss the verdict. They decide the six prisoners are guilty. The judge sentences the six men to seven years transportation.)

# Questions

**1 a** Why were the six Dorset labourers arrested?
  **b** Where were they put on trial?
  **c** What was their sentence?
  **d** Why did the government pardon the 'Tolpuddle Martyrs' in 1836?

**2** Use the dialogue to work out:
  **a** what evidence John Whetham might have given in court (you can assume his wife was telling the truth);
  **b** how the judge and the counsel for the prosecution summed up the case against the prisoners (use **A** as a guide).

**3 a** When does the judge interrupt court proceedings and why?
  **b** A judge is supposed to be *impartial* during a court hearing (ie. he

shouldn't take sides). Why, then, do you suppose Mr Justice Williams was so biased against the prisoners in the dock?

c  In what ways is George Loveless's account of the trial in **A** biased?

d  Why is it difficult to remain objective (unbiased) when studying a case like that of the Tolpuddle Martyrs?

e  In what way does the description of the men as 'martyrs' show bias?

f  Do you think the sentence given to the Tolpuddle Martyrs was fair? Give reasons for your answer.

**4** The following quotes are from newspapers which reported the Tolpuddle case. Would you say the quotes are biased in favour of the labourers or against them? Give reasons for your answers.

a  'Trade unions are, we have no doubt, the most dangerous institutions that were ever permitted to take root, under the shelter of the law in any country.' (*The Morning Post*)

b  'Trade associations should not be attacked by a verdict which shows the treachery of the law by throwing the noose of an Act of Parliament over the heads of sleeping men.' (*The Morning Herald*)

c  'A man is never punished in England for that which he is found guilty.' (*The Morning Chronicle*)

d  'The case represented an unreasonable and unacceptable stretching of an Act of Parliament. Our judges and law-makers may rely upon it, this case will never be forgotten.' (*The True Sun*)

# 3   Riots in 1886

In the last quarter of the nineteenth century Britain suffered a severe trade depression. From about 1875 both agriculture and industry went into decline. Unemployment rose and wages fell. The greatest sufferers from this depression were the unskilled workers. Some had to accept wage-cuts, others lost their jobs. There were protest meetings and demonstrations held all over the country. In February 1886 a large meeting of unemployed men was held in Trafalgar Square. The report (**A**) and the picture from *The Graphic* (**B**) describe how this meeting turned into a major riot.

> ❙ *The peace of the city has been disturbed this week (February 13) and property destroyed in a manner unknown to the residents of modern London. A great demonstration of the unemployed in Trafalgar Square on Monday was made use of by the leaders of the Revolutionary Social and Democratic Federation to repeat some of their recent and most violent attacks on the monied classes. An hour before the march arrived in Trafalgar Square, its approaches became crowded by a vast number of onlookers, estimated at from 15 000 to 20 000 in number. . . Fair traders, capitalists and Conservatives were denounced with great violence by the Social Democratic orators (speakers) at the north end of the square. Among them were Mr Burns and the notorious Mr Hyndman, the former declaring that at their next meeting the bakers' shops in the West End would be looted. After a good deal of speech-making, a large body of roughs made for Pall Mall where they smashed every window in the Carlton Club. Encouraged by their own numbers and the lack of policemen to be seen on their route, they smashed right and left the windows of the club-houses in St James's Street, up which they marched, turning into Piccadilly on their way to Hyde Park. By this time, probably some 2 000 strong, they began to get vicious. They hurled missiles at the inmates of passing carriages and dragged from them their lady occupants to be robbed of their ornaments. They also looted several shops, notably a jeweller's and a wine and spirit shop. In Hyde Park they halted to hear a few speeches from their leaders. Hyndman's words had little effect in restraining them. On making their way to South Audley Street, they smashed the windows along the line of route and attacked and plundered almost every shop in it – jewellers', drapers', butchers', poulterers', grocers' – using as missiles such*

1. BUSILY EMPLOYED—A SCENE IN THE STRAND
2. A SLIGHT POLITICAL DISAGREEMENT AT TRAFALGAR SQUARE
3. THE WAR OFFICE PROTECTED
4. " WHO STRIKES FIRST ? "

**C** The rioting in the West End of London, February 1886

*heavy objects as they did not care to carry away with them. The frightened shopkeepers seldom ventured to offer any resistance. Going through Grosvenor Square to North Audley Street, they plundered right and left and, reaching Oxford Street, stormed and looted several jewellers' shops. Meanwhile a body of police had been collected strong enough to confront them at Marylebone Lane, and to prevent further damage in Oxford Street shopkeepers hastily closed their premises. Then the ruffianly mob gradually melted away, leaving behind them memories of brutal violence and terrible destruction which will not easily be forgotten.* **(A)**

(*The Graphic*, 13 February 1886)

## Questions

**1 a** In which part of London were the meetings held?
 **b** Which political federation supported the meeting?
 **c** Name the leaders of the federation.
 **d** Where was the Carlton Club situated?

**2** What evidence is there in the sources to suggest:
  **a** that two separate demonstrations took place; **b** that social class was a political issue in 1886; **c** that the police mishandled the march?

**3 a** Which words or phrases in the written extract suggest that *The Graphic* was biased against the Social and Democratic Federation?
  **b** Why did *The Graphic* publish drawings of the demonstration rather than photographs?

**4** Using a street map around the Mayfair, Soho, Piccadilly area of London, work out the route taken by the marchers. Where did the police stop the march?

# 4  The match-girls' strike, 1888

Many of the trade unions which had grown up before 1870 had been for skilled or semi-skilled workers. During the 1870s and 1880s, unions for unskilled workers appeared. Between 1888 and 1889 there was a series of successful strikes amongst the lowest-paid unskilled and semi-skilled workers. The first strike was that of the London match-girls who worked for Bryant and May.

> ❠ *Our method of making matches is, I believe, perfectly free from any harmful influence upon the health of those engaged in it. We do not use the white or common phosphorus at all. The only phosphorus used is not in the match, but applied to the outside of the surface of the box, on which the match is rubbed, and this phosphorus is of the red kind, which is I believe perfectly harmless, and is not a poison. . . We find that we can always get as many hands as we require. It is not skilled labour, though some from practice will do three times the amount of others. . .* ❠  **(A)**
>
> (Quote from Mr William Bryant from Mr White's report on the Lucifer
> Match Manufacturer, 1863)

> ❠ *Promethean fire is afforded by the dipping process. At this point of the process the matches are double-headed and are twice as long as they ought to be. . . The 'boxers' empty the frames on a table. They then gather up a handful, place them in a grooved rest, and cut the mass in two with a short knife. One of these handfuls just goes into two boxes which the operators fill with amazing speed. One of the 'boxers' informs us that with steady working she could box 36 gross a day, that is to say 184 boxes. This girl earned 18 shillings a week. . . The workpeople are by no means the miserable, half-starved creatures whom some of our readers might expect to see. They were, as a rule, stout, ruddy, and well-dressed, and the younger children seemed full of spirit. At the same time one cannot help reflecting on the boredom of this form of factory labour. Fancy passing your whole earthly career in cutting up bundles of matches and then cramming them into boxes.* ❠  **(B)**
>
> (*The Graphic*, 20 May 1871)

**C** The match-makers at the East End, London

❝ *George Gardner, overlooker at Bryant & May's has worked in the business ever since he was 16. Dipped for 15 years of this time. Used to feel it in his chest very much. Thinks that was partly because he used to be out late and come in and lie down in the factory. That was very bad. Thinks partly too it was the sulphur dippings. That was very hot work. Used to get in a 'muck sweat' and then go out and catch cold. Has known many bad from the work. One lost his jaw. 'You could take his chin and shove it all into his mouth.' Has known several die from the 'phosphorus on their inwards.' Has known 18 or 20 lose their jaws. Has known 11 or 12 who have died from their jaw or their lungs. Other people might die of their lungs too. But the doctors said these had it from the phosphorus.*

*Cleanliness is the great thing. It is very important to wash; always did so himself after dipping. Used to wash out his mouth with water and 'goggle' his throat out. . . Some people are very dirty. One used to wash the basin for witness. Has seen him after this with his hand all plastered with the stuff eating his bread and butter. This man lost his jaw after two years. When dipping, witness used to blow away all the steam first and then breathe. So did all the rest. Used to put a piece of tobacco in his mouth; thought that was good. Is well now except he has a cough sometimes. Feels his chest then.*

*(Note. This witness does not look at all strong, and speaks feebly. He has all his teeth, though with many black places. He says they give no pain and thinks what looks like decay is the tobacco.)* **(D)**
(Government report on the match industry, 1875)

*Herbert Burrows and I interviewed some of the girls, got lists of wages, fines, etc. A typical case is that of a girl of 16, a piece-worker. She earns 4s (20p) a week and lives with a sister employed by the same firm who 'earns good money, as much as 8s (40p) or 9s (45p) a week.' Out of the earnings 2s (10p) a week is paid for the rent of one room. The child lives only on bread and butter and tea, alike for breakfast and dinner, but said that once a month she went for a meal where 'you get bread and butter and jam and marmalade and lots of it.' We published the facts in 'White Slavery in London', and called for a boycott of Bryant and May's matches.*

*I was immediately threatened with an action for libel but nothing came of it. It was easier to strike at the girls and a few days later Fleet Street was brought to life by a crowd of match-girls demanding to see Annie Besant. I asked that a delegation should come and explain what they wanted. Up came three women and told their story. They had been asked to sign a paper saying they were well-treated and happy, and that my article contained inaccurate facts. 'You had spoke up for us,' explained one, 'and we weren't going back on you.' A girl, chosen as their leader, was threatened with the sack. She stood firm. Next day she was discharged for some minor reason, and the girls all threw down their work, all 1 400 of them, and then a crowd of them started off to ask me what to do next. If ever we worked in our lives, we worked for the next fortnight. And a pretty hubbub we created. We asked for money, and it came pouring in. We registered the girls to receive strike pay, wrote articles, held public meetings, got Mr Bradlaugh to ask questions in Parliament, stirred up constituencies in which shareholders were members, till the whole country rang with the struggle.*

*The London Trades Council agreed to act as negotiators and an agreement was reached. The girls went into work, fines and deduc-*

*tions were abolished, better wages paid. The Matchmakers Union was set up, still the strongest women's trade union in England.* ❯ (E)

(From Annie Besant's *Autobiography*, 1893)

❮ *In 1888 the London match-girl workers of Bryant and May formed a union and struck for more pay and better conditions. Their complaints were very real for their wages were pitifully low (eight shillings a week for adults, four shillings for girls) and subject to fines. The work could be dangerous because of the sulphur which was not only highly inflammable but gave off poisonous fumes. Much of the work was also done on a domestic basis where there was ample opportunity for exploiting* (taking advantage of) *workers. Herbert Burrows and Annie Besant described their condition in an article called 'White Slavery in London', and called for a boycott of Bryant and May matches. The firm threatened legal action and forced the girls to sign a document stating they were well treated. One girl was sacked because she refused to sign it and 1 400 struck in protest. Annie Besant made public opinion fully aware of the plight of the workers; the appearance of the girls in the West End caused a sensation because of the state of their clothes and their unhealthy appearance. Finally, arbitrators settled the strike, and the firm was forced to end the system of fines, pay better wages and recognise the Match-girls' Union.* ❯ (F)

(R B Jones, *Economic and Social History of England*, 1971)

## Questions

**1** Use sources **A–F** to write your own account of the match-girls' strike. You should mention:
  **a** conditions of work and reasons for the strike;
  **b** the main events which took place during the strike;
  **c** the possible effects of the strike.

**2** Describe the feelings and reactions of each of the following people to news of the match-girls strike in 1888: a docker in the port of London; a banker working in the City of London; Mr William Bryant (the owner of the Lucifer Match Company).

**3** How did the match-girls' strike affect the development of other Trade Unions? (Use other sources and books to answer this question.)

# Section VI
# SOCIAL CHANGE

# 1 The poorhouse

Taunton is the county town of Somerset. The town lies in the centre of a rich farming area. In 1821, the parish of St Mary's was responsible for some of the town's poor. The list below (**A**) shows some of the 'food and sundreys' consumed by the paupers (poor people) in March 1821.

**A** Account of food in the poorhouse, March 24 to 30, 1821

# Questions

**1 a** During the week, how much money was spent on (i) cheese; (ii) sugar; (iii) thread? (Note: 12d=1s (5p) and 20s=£1)
**b** How much did one loaf of bread cost?
**c** How much was paid out in wages?

**2** Historians could use this list to work out what people ate in the poorhouse. If you were Betty Northcott and had been given the food in the list to cook, what meals would you have given the paupers? Draw up a timetable for breakfast, dinner and supper from Monday to Friday. (Note: for breakfast paupers usually had bread and cheese; for supper they often had bread and soup or bread and cheese.)

**3** Historians can also use a list like **A** to guess how healthy people were. Look at the vitamin chart below and then study **A** again.
**a** In which vitamins were the paupers lacking?
**b** If you had been a doctor in 1821, what diseases or disorders might you have found amongst the paupers?
**c** How does the food compare with what you eat most weeks?
**d** Can you think why those foods in particular were bought for the poor people?

| Vitamin | Found in: | Needed for: |
|---------|-----------|-------------|
| A | Carrots, egg yolks, butter, yellow or orange fruits, vegetables | Growth; prevention of dry skin; good eyesight |
| B | Wheat germ, bread, pork, liver, potatoes, milk, eggs | Good appetite and digestion; healthy skin |
| C | Fresh fruit and vegetables | Prevention of scurvy; good health; clear skin |
| D | Margarine, fish, oils, eggs, butter | Strong bones and teeth |
| K | Green vegetables | Clotting of blood |

**4 a** How could you use the list to work out the approximate number of people living in the poorhouse?
**b** What does the list tell us about (i) lighting; (ii) cleanliness; (iii) 'luxuries' in the poorhouse?
**c** If you were writing a history book about the Poor Law in 1821, what other primary sources would you want to refer to? What problems might you come across when using these sources?

# 2 The workhouse

The 1834 Poor Law Amendment Act set up a new system of poor relief. Poor people had to enter workhouses if they wished to receive help from the parish. The government appointed Boards of Guardians to supervise the running of the workhouses. The Boards paid officials to look after the poor. Conditions were made as harsh as possible to deter 'scroungers'.

In Taunton, Somerset, St Mary's Poorhouse (see previous chapter) was closed down. The inmates of the poorhouse were moved to a new union workhouse. The documents below describe conditions in the Taunton workhouse in 1840.

*Dietary for Able-Bodied Men and Women*

| | | Breakfast | | Dinner | | | | Supper | | |
|---|---|---|---|---|---|---|---|---|---|---|
| | | Bread | Gruel | Cooked Meat | Potatoes | Soup | Suet or Rice pudding | Bread | Cheese | Broth |
| | | oz | pints | oz | lb. | pints | oz | oz | oz | pints |
| Sunday | Men | 6 | 1½ | 4½ | 1 | " | " | 6 | " | 1½ |
| | Women | 5 | 1½ | 4½ | 1 | " | " | 5 | " | 1½ |
| Monday | Men | 6 | 1½ | " | 1 | 1½ | " | 6 | 1½ | " |
| | Women | 5 | 1½ | " | 1 | 1½ | " | 5 | 1½ | " |
| Tuesday | Men | 6 | 1½ | 4½ | 1 | " | " | 6 | " | 1½ |
| | Women | 5 | 1½ | 4½ | 1 | " | " | 5 | " | 1½ |
| Wednesday | Men | 6 | 1½ | " | 1 | 1½ | " | 6 | 1½ | " |
| | Women | 5 | 1½ | " | 1 | 1½ | " | 5 | 1½ | " |
| Thursday | Men | 6 | 1½ | 4½ | 1 | " | " | 6 | " | 1½ |
| | Women | 5 | 1½ | 4½ | 1 | " | " | 5 | " | 1½ |
| Friday | Men | 6 | 1½ | " | " | " | 14 | 6 | 1½ | " |
| | Women | 5 | 1½ | " | " | " | 12 | 5 | 1½ | " |
| Saturday | Men | 6 | 1½ | " | 1 | 1½ | " | 6 | 1½ | " |
| | Women | 5 | 1½ | " | 1 | 1½ | " | 5 | 1½ | " |

*Old People of 60 years of age and upwards may be allowed ¾ pint of tea*

**A** Dietary table for workhouse inmates

## DISCIPLINE AND DIET

XVI. As regards aged and infirm persons and children, the master and matron of the workhouse shall (subject to the directions of the Board of Guardians) fix such hours of rising and going to bed, and such occupation and employment as may be suitable to their respective ages and conditions.

XVII. The meals for the aged and infirm, the sick, and children, shall be provided at such times and in such manner as the Board of Guardians may direct.

XVIII. The boys and girls who are inmates of the workhouse shall, for three of the working hours, at least, every day, be respectively instructed in reading, writing, and principles of the Christian Religion, and such other instructions shall be imparted to them as are calculated to train them to habits of usefulness, industry, and virtue.

XIX. The diet of the paupers shall be so regulated as in no case to exceed in quantity and quality of food, the ordinary diet of the able-bodied labourers living within the same district.

XX. No pauper shall be allowed to have or use any wine, beer, or other spirituous or fermented liquors, unless by the direction in writing of the medical officer, who may also order for any individual pauper such change of diet as he shall deem necessary; and the master shall report such allowance or changes of diet so made, to the next meeting of Guardians, who may sanction, alter, or disallow the same at their discretion.

XXI. No pauper shall be allowed to work on his own account whilst an inmate of the workhouse; the Union which supports him being entitled to the full produce of his labour.

**B**  Discipline and diet in St Mary's Poorhouse

# Questions

**1** Which sources contain references to: **a** hours of work; **b** discipline; **c** food; **d** education in the workhouse?

**2 a**  Who were the Guardians (**B**) and what was their job?

 **b**  Why do you think a rigid system of diet (**A**) was drawn up?

**3** How does the diet in **A** compare with that described on page 150? What does this tell us about changes in the Poor Law between 1821 and 1840?

**4** Use both the sources to describe a typical day in the workhouse in about 1840.

# 3  The state of the towns

Britain was the first country in the world to have an industrial revolution. Its greatest impact was on parts of the country which had supplies of iron and coal needed for the steam engine. Between 1750 and 1840 new towns sprang up in South Wales, the West Midlands, South Lancashire and the West Riding of Yorkshire. In these growing towns overcrowding was probably the biggest single cause of bad conditions. Problems such as slum housing, bad health, poverty, crime and poor working conditions became much more serious. Villages were turned into cities, streams and rivers became open sewers, grey buildings swallowed up fields, cart tracks became roads. Town centres became slum areas squeezed tightly between factories and mills. Well-to-do citizens left the town centres and built themselves homes in the new suburbs or the country.

In 1842 Edwin Chadwick, a lawyer and social reformer, produced a report on *The Sanitary Condition of the Labouring Population of Great Britain*. The report revealed appalling living conditions throughout the country. MPs realised that something would have to be done to clean up Britain's growing towns and cities. In 1843 Robert Peel's government appointed a Royal Commission to check the facts in Chadwick's report and to examine his recommendations. The dialogue below is based on evidence given to this commission in 1843.

**The commissioners**

Robert Stephenson – Railway engineer
James Smith – Agricultural engineer
John Playfair – Chemist
William Cubitt – Civil Engineer
David Reid – Ventilation expert

**The witnesses**

William Thorn – Refuse collector
Dr John Liddle – Medical officer of the Whitechapel Union
Samuel Moore – President of the Agricultural Society of Manchester

**Scene:** Gwydr House, Whitehall, London. A cold spring day in 1843.

Stephenson : *Are we therefore agreed that we listen to Thorn's evidence first?*
Playfair : *That seems a sensible arrangement.*
(Enter William Thorn)
Stephenson : *Mr Thorn, can you let the Commission know exactly what sort of work you do?*
Thorn : *Certainly. I'm the cleansing contractor for refuse and dust collection in the south-western district of St Pancras and the St Mary's division of Marylebone.*

| | | |
|---|---|---|
| Stephenson | : | *Is it true that you've been finding difficulty in locating places where filth may be deposited in the busier parts of London?* |
| Thorn | : | *The problem is that very few people in London want to live anywhere near a place in which muck is stored.* |
| Cubitt | : | *Is there not a great increase of buildings in the London area which are gradually covering over those places which used to be used for depositing filth?* |
| Thorn | : | *Yes, the builders are gradually driving us out.* |
| Stephenson | : | *Surely local people object to you dumping filth in their neighbourhood?* |
| Thorn | : | *Yes. They say they do not like our men and they do not like the carts carrying the muck. We are not a very pleasant sort of people.* |
| Reid | : | *The ashes and breeze* (cinders) *you collect are used to make bricks. What happens to the . . . er . . . other stuff?* |
| Thorn | : | *If we mix the street-sweepings with the horse-dung and cow-dung, we get rid of it to the farmers, who use it for fallow lands for manuring, for turnips and wheat, and all their produce in fact. If we sell it alone without mixing it with horse-dung and cow-dung, it is put on meadow land after the first crop of hay is off.* |
| Playfair | : | *Do you also carry night-soil – the contents of privvies and cess-pools?* |
| Thorn | : | *We have one place to which we can carry it, over the canal bridge, about 500 yards on the same road. We lay it down in the middle of a very large field. The person who allows us to dump it there, Mr Clarke, bakes it, I believe and sends it over to the West Indies.* |
| Cubitt | : | *What is the average cost of cleaning out a cess-pool?* |
| Thorn | : | *It is done by the load. Our average is usually ten shillings a one-horse and 15 shillings a two-horse load. A load is about a cubic yard. The houses we are most in the habit of removing night-soil from are lodging-houses with a family on every floor. That is about five loads. We cleanse those once a year, or once in eighteen months. During the last 13 weeks of the St Giles contract we were paid five shillings a week for keeping the inhabitants in Lascelles Court, Holborn, decent. They were using a small place for a privy which had seemed to have originally been a sentry box and what a place of filth it was!* |
| Cubitt | : | *So these people had no proper privy at all?* |
| Thorn | : | *No. At that time they threw all their refuse into the muck and made it worthless. We were paying a large sum for the dust and it was a great loss to us.* |
| Smith | : | *How do you get rid of the bones and those things?* |
| Thorn | : | *Our general plan is to contract. We underlet our work of sifting to a man. He gets the ashes and bones and other things. We keep the oyster shells, he sells the bones. The bones are always sold to the Jews. They send them away in barges and they are taken and boiled, I believe, and used as bone-dust for manure. The rags are washed. If they are any good, they are taken to the papermills and used for making paper. The woollen rags are taken into the country and laid down till they moulder away and then the rag-dust is sold to the hop-farmers in Kent. It is an excellent thing to prevent the fly in wine. Oyster-shells, broken crockery and everything that we call 'hard core' is sold to the contractors for roads.* |
| Reid | : | *Do you pay extra wages to the men who get the night soil?* |
| Thorn | : | *Yes, we pay so much a load to the men. For a fair night-job we send out five men and a cart, and I generally send a foreman with them. I do not like such a thing as spilling it on the road or the men getting drunk. We pay the men 6d a load to each of the five men, and for* |

an average job that is 2/6d to each man. For that they work till five in the morning, or not quite as long. You see most of the work must be done by four o'clock.

| | | |
|---|---|---|
| Reid | : | *Are they paid more because the work is so disagreeable?* |
| Thorn | : | *Yes, they get a third more, at least.* |
| Stephenson | : | *Do they drink a great deal?* |
| Thorn | : | *Yes. It is a very disagreeable job. I do not wonder at their drinking. They come in as lads. They come in from the country and once they get into a nightman's yard, they never leave it. We have got a man now that is 67. They live to a good age in general.* |
| Stephenson | : | *Thank you, Mr Thorn.* |

*(Thorn goes out)*

| | | |
|---|---|---|
| Playfair | : | *I'm not sure how much we can rely upon Thorn's evidence. After all, he's got a vested interest in refuse and dust collection.* |
| Stephenson | : | *I don't know. Most of what he said seemed to ring true. However, let's hear Moore next. He should be able to tell us what things are like in Manchester.* |

*(Enter Samuel Moore)*

| | | |
|---|---|---|
| Stephenson | : | *Mr Moore, what can you tell us about the disposal of refuse and filth in Manchester?* |
| Moore | : | *It's pretty bad all round. The neglected state of courts and alleys has resulted in a practice unknown outside of Lancashire. People place their refuse and muck in open cesspits, dunghills or 'middens' in the centre of the courts. And there is no organised system of removing the mess. This has led to the existence in large towns of a wretched set of men. . .* |
| Smith | : | *Don't tell me. The nightmen?* |
| Moore | : | *Aye. And the nightmen of Manchester are filthy in their appearance and habits. They're often helped out by their families and their houses are the most disgusting places imaginable.* |
| Reid | : | *How much are they paid?* |
| Moore | : | *They get three shillings for a load of two tons. To obtain this quantity, two men with the help of their families may be able to load two carts from 3 am to 9 am. They therefore go to the places where most manure can be obtained using the least labour. Some places never get cleaned out.* |
| Reid | : | *And what do the local people think of the nightmen?* |
| Moore | : | *Most townspeople visited by this rough lot consider them a damned nuisance – excuse the language. Many of the privvies are damaged and made useless by the nightmen. Sometimes they break up the floors and seats to get out the soil. Some of them pull down one side of the bog-hole so that their work is made easier. So they cause considerable damage to property. The privvies are left in a disgusting state for a long time. The place becomes a mass of filth as the days pass and more and more muck piles up.* |
| Reid | : | *This gets worse and worse! It looks as if Chadwick was right.* |
| Stephenson | : | *Thank you, Mr Moore, we have no further questions.* |

*(Moore goes out)*

| | | |
|---|---|---|
| Reid | : | *This is getting rather depressing.* |
| Stephenson | : | *Well, we only have time for one more witness this afternoon. John Liddle has kindly agreed to come along to talk to us about er. . . water supply. It seems to me we'll never make improvements in health and sanitation without supplies of clean, pure water.* |

(Enter John Liddle)

| | | |
|---|---|---|
| Stephenson | : | *Mr Liddle, how would you describe the living conditions of the mass of the working-class people in Whitechapel?* |
| Liddle | : | *Truly appalling.* |
| Cubitt | : | *And the water supply?* |
| Liddle | : | *Water is laid on to very few houses. Most people get their water from a plug (hole) in the courts. I can't say whether it is the lack of water or people's unwillingness to fetch it, but the effect is a shortage of water. When I have visited their rooms, they have very little water in their tubs. When they are washing, the smell of the dirt mixed with the soap is quite disgusting. They merely pass dirty linen through very dirty water. The smell of the linen when so washed is very offensive and must have a bad effect on the health of the people there. The filth in their houses is dreadful, so is their personal filth.* |
| Playfair | : | *This must create a disgusting smell.* |
| Liddle | : | *When they come to my surgery, I always have to keep the door open. When I am coming down stairs from the parlour, I know at a distance whether there are any poor patients in the surgery.* |
| Playfair | : | *And how do the poor get rid of their dirty water?* |
| Liddle | : | *When I come to think of it, I do not think there is one house in working-class districts in which there is such a thing as a sink for getting rid of the water. And there is no such thing in the poorer places as a house with water laid on. There is also a shortage of cess-pools. There is only one or two cess pools for a whole court and soil lies around the places which are in a most offensive condition.* |
| Smith | : | *And you would say that these public nuisances are one cause of the high death rate in Whitechapel?* |
| Liddle | : | *Most certainly.* |
| Stephenson | : | *And what happens to the corpse when someone dies?* |
| Liddle | : | *The problem is that nearly the whole of the labouring population in Whitechapel have only one room. The corpse is therefore kept in that room where people sleep and have their meals. Sometimes the corpse is stretched on the bed, and the bed and bedclothes are taken off, and the wife and the family lie on the floor. When children die, they are often laid out on the table.* |
| Smith | : | *How long does the corpse remain in the house?* |
| Liddle | : | *It varies according to the day of the death. Sunday is the day usually chosen for the day of burial. But if a man dies on the Wednesday, the funeral will not take place till the Sunday the week following. Bodies are almost kept for a full week, sometimes longer.* |
| Cubitt | : | *What do the family do. . .how do they cope while the corpse is lying there?* |
| Liddle | : | *What I see when I first visit the room is an attitude of indifference to the corpse being there. The family is found eating or drinking or getting on with their usual business, and the children playing. Amongst the middle classes, where there is more opportunity of putting the corpse by itself, there are greater marks of respect and decency. Among that class no one would think of doing anything in the room where the corpse was lying, still less allowing children there.* |
| Smith | : | *I must say, I find this quite shocking.* |
| Stephenson | : | *Thank you, Mr. Liddle.* |

(Liddle goes out)

*I suppose we'd better start on our report. How shall we begin?*

# Questions

**1 a** Make a list of four major dangers to the health of people in towns mentioned by the witnesses.
**b** Who were the 'night men' and why were they often heavy drinkers?
**c** How did refuse collection in Manchester and London differ?
**d** How were rags, bones and oyster-shells re-cycled?

**2 a** How do you think the five commissioners who took part in the inquiry were chosen?
**b** Which of the witnesses gave the least reliable evidence and why?
**c** How could the commissioners have checked that the information given by the witnesses was accurate?
**d** If you had been a member of the commission, what other questions would you have put to Thorn, Liddle and Moore?

**3** What do you think the commission finally recommended in its report? In groups, discuss the evidence given by the witnesses. Then draw up a list of six recommendations you would wish to see implemented by the government. Your group should place these recommendations in order of importance.

# 4 Cholera

Cholera was one of the most frightening diseases of the nineteenth century. It did not kill more people than other diseases but it struck with sudden and horrifying force. There were serious cholera outbreaks in Britain in 1831–2, 1838, 1848–9 and 1854.

The germs which cause cholera are found in the excreta of people who have caught the disease. The spread of cholera over a wide area was usually caused by these germs getting into drinking water. It spread quickly because sewage was pumped into rivers and the same water was later used for drinking. When this happened, so many people caught the disease that an epidemic (the sudden outbreak of a disease which sweeps through the country and then dies away) started.

Sources **A–D** describe how doctors, Poor Law Boards and Public Health Boards tried to limit the spread of cholera in Somerset in 1848.

❝ *The Vice-Chairman reported that several cases of cholera broke out yesterday in some cottages in Monmouth Street belonging to Mr Mogg. Mr Parker, Vice-Chairman, made known to the Board that Mr King, Medical Officer of the workhouse, had informed him that he had found some difficulty in obtaining proper attendance on the sick patients, particularly as regards a patient labouring under cholera, the nurse being fearful of treating the patient. . . The nurse was called in who stated that she was not at all afraid of the complaint, that she had sat up all night, and that she had last night visited her every half hour, upon which the Board expressed themselves satisfied. . . Mr King was called in. He made no complaint against the nurse but said that he had experienced difficulty in obtaining help from the workhouse inmates. The Master stated that if the Board would allow the inmates extra food, there would be no further difficulties. It was resolved that the master be instructed to give the pauper inmates attending sick patients such extra food as the Medical Officer directed.*

*It being considered desirable to obtain possession of the Bridgwater Parish Workhouse as a cholera hospital, it was resolved that the sum of £20 be granted for that purpose. Mr Hayward, the occupier of the house was sent for.*

*Six deaths had occurred and from the state of the cottages the Vice-Chairman had felt it his duty to remove some of the inhabitants to the Old Poor House and other children who were in a healthy state were removed to the union that they might be out of the way of infection. He had also ordered that extra food be sent to the Old Poor House. . . Mr Parker, the Medical Officer, reported to the Board that he considered the removal of the children to the Union House most providential. . . Mr Hayward agreed to give up immediate possession of the house upon condition of the Board's paying him £20 as compensation for the inconvenience.*

*Ordered – that the House be immediately whitewashed and put in order for the reception of patients.*

*The Board adjourned to 12 o'clock, Monday 1 October.*  (A)

(Minutes from a meeting of the Bridgwater Poor Law Board, 1848)

## Questions

**1** Look at **B**.

**a** If you want to avoid cholera, what advice does Marwood give you about **(i)** food; **(ii)** clothing; **(iii)** 'sanitary measures'?

**b** How does the local Board of Health intend to help?

**2** Using both of the sources answer the following.

**a** What measures did the authorities take to stop the spread of cholera?

**b** How effective do you think these measures were?

**c** What sort of medicines were recommended?

**d** What did doctors believe was the cause of cholera?

**e** We now know that cholera is usually spread by contaminated water. Does either source refer to polluted water?

**f** If you had been a Medical Officer of Health in 1848, what measures would you have taken to stop the spread of cholera in your area?

# CAUTIONARY
# NOTICE!!

Some cases of Cholera having appeared at the Union Workhouse, to which the disease is at present confined, the Local Board of Health desire to impress on the Public that the progress and fatal effects of this disease may be controlled to a very great extent indeed, by prompt preventive measures, and the Board call upon the inhabitants to co-operate with them in their endeavours to avert the threatened destruction of human life.

The Town will forthwith be divided into districts, each district being under the charge of appointed persons, who will visit from House to House, who will insist on the removal of everything prejudicial to health, as far as practicable, and the adoption of thorough cleansing—white-liming and ventilation. Enquiry will also be constantly made as to the health of the inmates, their house accommodation, and other circumstances connected with the object.

Individuals are recommended to live as generously as they are able, but they are cautioned to be careful not to indulge in intemperance—not to meet in crowded, heated rooms, not to keep late hours—and to avoid *all tainted* and indigestible food, and sleeping in overcrowded bed-chambers.

Warm clothing, washing the surface of the body with tepid salt and water, followed by dry rubbing, is advised, also, the free use of fresh Common Table Salt, a tea-spoonful of which should be taken at breakfast, two at dinner, and one at tea or supper. A proportionate quantity, say one-third or one-half, may be given to children, according to age. A less dose should be resorted to *at first*, if it offend the stomach.

The immediate use of Sir W. Burnett's disinfecting fluid, or Collins's Powder is advised in crowded and unfavourable situations.

Should the slightest symptom of disturbance of the stomach or bowels occur, either *with* or *without* pain, *instant* application should be made for medical help. *Medicines are supplied gratis at the Hospital.*

The Local Board of Health rely on the ready co-operation of the inhabitants in the adoption of every available protective measure. The surest way to restore confidence and to lessen unnecessary and hurtful alarm is to shew that the Town is prepared for an emergency should it arise. The Board are resolved to enforce the humane provisions of the Public Health Act, and seconded in their endeavours by the inhabitants, they have no doubt that under Providence the progress of disease will be arrested. The experience *of all other places* justifies such a conclusion.

N.B.—It is requested that Notice be immediately given to Mr. SAMUEL POLLARD, Inspector of Nuisances, if any unwholesome food should be offered for Sale, that persons so offending may be immediately proceeded against.

### *By Order of the Board,*
# WM. MARWOOD, Clerk.

Taunton, November 5, 1849.          WOODLEY, PRINTER, GAZETTE OFFICE, TAUNTON.

**B** Taunton notice about cholera, 1848

# 5  Rats in the sewers

Henry Mayhew (1812–1887) was the son of a London solicitor. In the 1840s he became a journalist and social investigator. By 1849 he was writing articles about slum housing, working conditions and cholera outbreaks for the *Morning Chronicle*, a daily newspaper. In 1851 Mayhew published *London Labour and the London Poor*, one of the most famous surveys of Victorian poverty. In this book he tried to show how low-paid working people coped with poverty and ill-health. The extract below reflects Mayhew's concern about dangerous working conditions and public health.

❛ *In the better-constructed sewers there are no rats. In the old sewers there are thousands. The sewer-rat is the ordinary house or brown rat, except at the outlets near rivers, and here the water-rat is seen. . . The rat is the only animal found in the sewers. I met with no flushermen* (men who cleaned out the sewers) *who had ever seen a lizard, frog or toad there. A few live cats find their way into underground channels when a house-drain is being built or is opened for repairs, and have been seen by the flushermen wandering about, looking lost, mewing in misery and avoiding any contact with the sewage. The rats also – for they are not of the water-rat breed – are greatly averse to wetting their feet, and 'take to the sewage' only when faced with danger; that is, they then swim along the current to escape with their lives. It is said that when an unlucky cat has wandered into the sewers, she is sometimes attacked by the rats. An honest flusherman said that a few years back he had in one week found the skeletons of two cats in a particular part of an old sewer, 21 feet wide, and in the drains beside them were thousands of rats, raging with hunger. Some of the fur was still attached to the skeletons but the flesh had all been eaten away. About that time a troop of rats flew at the feet of another of my informants but his boots 'stopped the devils'. 'The sewers generally swarm with rats,' said another man. 'I runs away from them; they in general gets away from us. But if we come to a stunt-end where part of the sewer is blocked off, and we goes to touch them, they fly at us. Some of them are as big as good-sized kittens. One of our men caught hold of one the other day by the tail, and the tail slipping through his fingers, he put up his left hand to stop it, and the rat caught hold of his finger, and the man's got an arm now as big as his thigh.'*

*'Why, sir,' said one flusherman, 'as to the number of rats, it ain't possible to say. There hasn't been a census taken of them. But I can tell you this – I was one of the first flushermen when flushing came in general – I think it was before Christmas, 1847, under Mr Roe – and there was cart-loads and cart-loads of drowned rats carried into the Thames. But now I see far fewer drowned rats now than before the shores were flushed.'*

*The rats do not get much food from the matter in the sewers, or only from certain sewers. These are the sewers beneath the slaughter-houses at Newgate Market or Smithfield. Animal offal is swept into the drains and sewers, and there the rats find all their food. In the sewers, generally, there is little food for them, and none at all in the best constructed sewers, where there is a regular and rapid flow, and little or no deposit.*

*The sewers are these animals' breeding grounds. In them the broods are usually safe from predators like man, dogs or cats. These breeding grounds are sometimes in the holes which have been formed in the old sewers by a crumbled brick having fallen out. Their nests, however, are in some parts even more frequent in places where old rotting house-drains or smaller sewers, empty themselves into a first-class sewer. Here, then, the rats breed, and find their way up the drains or pipes, even through the openings into water-closets, into the houses for their food and almost always at night. One man gave me this account of a rat settlement: 'Why, sir, in the Milford Lane sewer, I've seen and reported what was a regular chamber of rats. I couldn't get into the rat-hole but I've brought my lamp to the opening and*

**B** Rat-catcher in a London sewer 1851

*have seen it plain. I should say, that it was the size of a small room, at least six yards by four. I've sometimes heard the rats squeaking and fighting there, like a parcel of drunken Irishmen. Some of them were rare big fellows. I should say there were over 300 rats in that small room. If a poor cat strayed in there, she wouldn't tackle the rats, not she. There's lots of such places, sir, here, there and everywhere.* **(A)**

(Henry Mayhew, *London Labour and the London Poor*, 1851–2)

**C** Jack Black, Her Majesty's rat-catcher

**D** London sewer 1854

# Questions

**1 a** What sort of rats lived in a Victorian sewer?
  **b** What happened to cats which wandered into rat-infested sewers?
  **c** What did the rats eat?
  **d** How did the rats find their way into people's homes?

**2 a** What do **B** and **D** tell you about the construction of 19th century sewers and the men who worked there?
  **b** Source **C** shows 'Jack Black', Her Majesty's rat-catcher. Describe his appearance. Why was a royal rat-catcher necessary?

**3 a** Why do you think there were no rats in the 'better-constructed' sewers?
  **b** Can you think of a reason why rat-catchers went down sewers to obtain live rats?
  **c** What sort of diseases are carried by rats?

**4** Use the sources and your own knowledge of the topic to explain why rats and other vermin became less of a menace to public health in the second half of the nineteenth century. You could mention: Public Health Acts; better houses; new sewers; sanitation; refuse disposal; street cleaning; education; medical advances; poisons.

# 6  Climbing boys

The working children who attracted the most attention in the nineteenth century were the 'climbing boys' who worked for chimney sweeps. Many of these were children in the care of the parish but some came from private homes. The children were supposed to become apprentices to the working chimney sweeps but some master sweeps treated their apprentices little better than slaves. The apprentices were forced to climb narrow, twisting chimneys about 23 cm square to clean them out. The soot often caused cancer and many boys died at an early age.

Between 1778 and 1875 men like Jonas Hanway, Charles Dickens and Lord Shaftesbury tried to persuade Parliament to pass laws banning the use of climbing boys. Henry Mayhew (see p. 162) wrote articles like **A** describing the lifestyle of working sweeps. In 1875 a boy of 14 died after sweeping a chimney at an asylum near Cambridge. *The Times* newspaper launched a public campaign against the master sweep responsible for the boy's death. In 1875 Parliament passed an Act which stated that all chimney sweeps had to be licensed. Licences were issued only to sweeps not using climbing boys.

**6** *Chimney-sweepers have long been looked down upon as the lowest order of workers. The nature of their work gives them not only a filthy appearance, but an offensive smell. Their numbers were, in the days of climbing boys, increased by parish apprentices. The climbing boys were almost always cruelly used, starved, beaten, and overworked by their masters, and treated as outcasts by all with whom they came in contact.*

*Speaking of the men generally, I am assured that there is scarcely one out of ten who can either read or write. One man in Chelsea informed me that some ladies, in connection with the Rev. Mr Cadman's church, made an attempt to instruct the sweepers of the neighbourhood in reading and writing; but the master sweepers grew jealous, and became afraid lest their men should get too knowing for them. The masters always managed to find out some job which prevented the men from attending at the appointed time, and the consequence was that the designs of the ladies were frustrated.*

*The sweepers, as a class, in almost all their habits, bear a strong resemblance to the costermongers* (men who sold fruit and fish from barrows in the street). *The better-class sweepers have risen to be masters, and, becoming settled in an area, have gradually obtained the trade of the neighbourhood; then, as their circumstances improved, they have been able to get horses and carts, and become nightmen emptying privies; and there are many of them at this moment men of wealth.*

*The ordinary sweepers are, in the main, addicted to drinking, beer being their favourite drink, either because it is the cheapest or because they believe that it is suitable for washing away the soot which finds its way to their throats. The men gamble as well but seldom play for money. They spend their time and what money they have in tossing for beer, till they are either drunk or penniless. Such men look as if they have just come out of a chimney. There never seems to be any attempt made by them to wash the soot off their faces. I am informed that hardly any of them have a second shirt, or any change of clothes, and that they wear their garments night and day till they literally rot and drop in fragments from their backs. Those who are not able to find work are frequently whole days without food, especially in summer, when the work is slack. Washing among chimney-sweepers seems to be much more frequent than it was. In the evidence before Parliament it was stated that some of the climbing-boys were washed once in six months, some once a week, some once in two or three months. I do not find it anywhere stated that any of these children were never washed at all; but it may reasonably be concluded that such was the case. A master sweeper, who was in the habit of bathing at the Marylebone baths, assured me that although many now eat and drink and sleep sooty, washing is more common among his class than when he himself was a climbing-boy. He used then to be stripped, and forced into a tub, and into water sometimes too hot and sometimes too cold, while his mistress scoured him. The master sweeper was certain that 30 or 40 years ago climbing-boys were rarely washed; and then it was looked upon as a most disagreeable operation, indeed as a type of punishment. Some of the climbing boys were taken by their masters to bathe in the Serpentine many years ago; but one boy was unfortunately drowned, so that few children wanted to go into the water afterwards.*

**B**  Soot covered climbing boys at supper

*The sweepers in general are, I am assured, fond of oleaginous (greasy) food; fat broth, faggots, and 'greasy' meat. Many of these men suffer from the chimney sweep's cancer, which is said to arise from uncleanly habits. Some sweepers assure me that they have vomited balls of soot.* **(A)**

(Henry Mayhew, *London Labour and the London Poor*, 1851)

**C**  One of the few remaining chimney sweeps in 1850

# Questions

**1 a**  Why are chimney-sweeps 'looked down upon as the lowest order of workers'?

  **b**  Why did an attempt to educate chimney-sweeps fail?

  **c**  What sort of work did 'costermongers' do?

**2 a**  Describe the sweeps' home in **B**.

  **b**  According to Mayhew's evidence in **A**, what sort of food are the boys in **B** likely to be eating and drinking?

  **c**  **C** shows a climbing chimney-sweep in about 1850. Why do you think that by this date there were very few 'climbing men' still working in our towns and cities?

  **d**  What sort of personal qualities would you need to be a 'climbing man'?

**e** What evidence is there in **A** to suggest that Mayhew carried out face-to-face interviews with chimney-sweeps? How reliable does this make **A**?

**3** Use the source material from this chapter and any other information you can find to explain why Parliament restricted the use of climbing boys in 1875.

# 7 A visit to Whitechapel in 1872

Gustave Doré (1832–1883) was one of the most famous artists and engravers of the nineteenth century. Doré, a Frenchman, specialised in producing drawings which could later be engraved on wooden blocks by teams of craftsmen. In 1872 Doré and his friend Blanchard Jerrold visited London. The two friends travelled round Whitechapel, a poverty-stricken area in the East End of London (**A**). They were accompanied by a plain-clothes detective. Jerrold made notes of the visit and Doré drew rough sketches of what he saw (**B** and **C**). The sketches were later turned into engravings. These pictures were considered to be so accurate that they were later used to illustrate government reports. They give historians a vivid picture of what city life was like in the latter part of the last century.

> ❝We rattled through dark lanes, across horrid, flashing highways, to the Whitechapel Police Station, to pick up the superintendent of savage London. We dismiss our cab; it would be useless in the dark, strange streets to which we are bound. The missionary, the rent collector, the policeman, the detective and the undertaker are the human beings who appear in the weird and horrible Bluegate Fields; where in the open doorways low-browed ruffians and women scowl

at us as we pass, keeping carefully in the middle of the road. 'Stick close together gentlemen; this is a rough part,' our careful guides tell us – some walking before, others behind – the local superintendent or the Scotland Yard sergeant accosting each policeman on his beat, and now and then collecting two or three, and planting them at strategic points or openings, that cover our advance, and keep the country open behind us.

We plunge into a maze of courts and narrow streets of low houses – nearly all the doors of which are open, showing kitchen fires blazing far in the interior, and strange figures moving about. Whistles, shouts, oaths, growls, and the brazen laughter of drunken women: sullen 'good nights' to the police; black pools of water under our feet – only a slither of violet grey sky overhead! We come to a halt at a low black door. The superintendent's knock means immediate opening. An old man in corduroy breeches and grey stockings, unbuttoned waist-coat and dirty shirt-sleeves – with a low cap over his eyes, is about to growl when the 'Good night, Ben,' of the force, brings him to attention and respect at once.

We advance into a low, long, dark room parted into boxes, in which are packed the most evil company any great city could show. They stare, leer, dig each other in the ribs, and grunt and growl as the superintendent reviews them. The place is clean, compared with the guests, thanks to the Common Lodging House Act; but it is charged with the damp and mouldy smell that is in every thieves' kitchen, in every common lodging house, every ragged hotel. We pass from kitchen to kitchen and from lodging to lodging, up and down two or three lanes; threading the long passages of thin boards that separate the twopenny beds of the lodgers, and here and there coming upon heart-breaking scenes of disease and helplessness. In one box an old man is dying of asthma; in another two fine baby boys cling together, sleeping until their mother brings them home some supper from the hard streets. People crowd upon us with imploring or threatening eyes from under the rags hanging over the kitchen fire; from foggy corners where they are eating scraps; from benches where they are playing push-penny. Men and women, girls and boys, all quarrelling or rollicking together: the flower-seller with the thief, the virtuous girl and the hussy. From low house to low house we go, picking up some fresh scrap of the history of poverty and crime – they must go hand-in-hand at every turn. At dark corners, lurking men keep close to the wall, and the police smile when we wonder what would become of a wanderer lost in these regions. 'He would be stripped to his shirt,' was the answer while we threaded our way through a maze of dark alleys. We were on our way to the dreadful paved court in which our old friend the Lascar (an Indian sailor) rolled upon his mattress stirring his stifling opium over a lamp.

We turned into one of the lowest of low lodging houses. It was a small kitchen, with two or three hideous old hags in it – and a child covered in dirt, rolling on the hearth. A bull's eye (policeman's lamp) was turned upon the landlady – she was shamefaced and tried to hide her bruised arms and cheeks. The child had got upon its legs – and while it held one hand towards us, begging, it clawed the drunken mother's arm with the other and grinned in her sheepish face. We were introduced to the room in which 'Edwin Drood' (a novel by Charles Dickens) opens. Upon the wreck of a four-post

**B**  Opium smoking – the Lascar's room in *Edwin Drood*

bedstead, upon a mattress heaped with dusty clothes, lay a sprawling Lascar, dead drunk with opium; and at the foot of the bed sat a woman, with a little brass lamp among the rags covering her, stirring the opium. She turned her head dreamily as we entered. She shivered under the gust of night air we had brought in, and went on warming the black mixture. It was difficult to see any humanity in that face, as the enormous grey dry lips lapped the rough wood pipe and drew in the poison. The man looked dead. She said he had been out since four in the morning trying to get a job in the docks – and had failed.

**C** Wentworth Street, Whitechapel

*We escaped from the opium fumes, in which a score of white mice (the woman's pets) were running over the rags and dirt she called her bed; back through the tangle of courts to the casual ward of St George-in-the-East, where we knocked up an old pauper who was keeping the fire alight in the deserted oakum shed; signed our names; peeped in at the rows of vagrants sleeping, rolled up like mummies, and went home gradually, by the flaming lights of Shadwell. Demands for gin came from all sides. Women old and young, girls and boys in tattered clothes; even the Fire-King who was performing before half a dozen sailors, and the pot-boy who showed the way up the steep stairs – all wanted gin, nothing but gin. Some cried for a pint, others for half a pint, others for a glass: not so much because they had any hope that their prayer would be granted, as mocking us for witnessing their condition. Rebuked (told off) by the police, they would fall back and make faces at us, and imitate our manners, our voices, our movements.* **(A)**

(Gustave Doré and Blanchard Jerrold, *London, A Pilgrimage*, 1872)

# Questions

**1** Who or what were: a 'bull's eye'; a 'lascar'; 'Edwin Drood'; 'courts'?

**2 a** For what reasons do you think Doré and Jerrold decided to visit Whitechapel in 1872?
**b** Describe in detail what you can see in **B** and **C**.
**c** What ideas about Whitechapel did Doré want to convey in these pictures?

**3 a** What sort of people could be seen in Bluegate Fields (**A**)? What does this tell us about the area?
**b** Where, in the written extract, can you find references to: (**i**) parliamentary legislation; (**ii**) unemployment; (**iii**) narcotic (drug) abuse; (**iv**) alcoholism; (**v**) child-abuse?
**c** Which sentence in the written extract suggests that some inhabitants of Whitechapel corrupted (had a bad influence on) others?
**d** 'The history of poverty and crime ... must go hand-in-hand at every turn.' (**A**) In your own words, explain what this means.

**4** Pictures like **B** and **C** were used to illustrate a government report on poverty in the East End. Use **A** and any other information you can find to write the part of the report which might have accompanied **B** and **C**.

# Section VII
# REVISION

# 1 Robert Morvinson

**A** Robert Morvinson (1775–1865)

Photograph **A** was taken in 1857. Robert Morvinson was a carrier and shoemaker from Stallingborough, Lincolnshire. Morvinson was 82 when this photograph was taken. He died at the age of 90.

In the year Morvinson was born Britain had a sluggish economy and farming practices had changed very little since medieval times. In the year he died, Britain was at the peak of its industrial and agricultural prosperity and at the height of its military power.

## Questions

**1** Copy and complete the timeline shown on the next page to show some of the major historical events which took place during Robert Morvinson's life. Write the important dates in the left-hand column and the events in the appropriate right-hand column. Some of the dates and events have been put in for you. You will need a reference book or your GCSE textbook to help you with this exercise.

**2** Which events on your timeline do you think Morvinson himself would have regarded as most important? Why?

**3** Design a similar timeline to show the most important events which have taken place during your lifetime.

| Date | Agriculture | Industry | Transport | Social change | Politics |
|------|-------------|----------|-----------|---------------|----------|
| 1775 | | Watt and Boulton in partnership | | | |
| ? | | | | | Gordon Riots |
| ? | | 'Puddling and Rolling' | John Palmer's mail coaches | Wesley ordains his own ministers | General election |
| ? | | Cartwright's power loom | | | |
| ? | Speenhamland system | | 'Canal Mania' | | |
| ? | | | First steamship launched | | Peace of Amiens |
| 1805 | | | | | ? |
| ? | | | | British slave trade abolished | |
| ? | | | 'Catch-me-who-can' | | Peninsular War begins |
| ? | | Luddite activity | | | |
| ? | | | Stephenson's 'Blücher' | | Abdication of Napoleon |
| 1815 | ? | Miner's safety lamp | | | ? |
| ? | | | | Factory Act | 'Peterloo' Riots |
| 1820 | | | | | George IV |
| ? | | | Rainhill Trials | Metropolitan Police | |
| ? | Corn Law sliding scale | | | Mines Act/ Chadwick's Report | Second Chartist petition |
| ? | Swing Riots | | Liverpool and Manchester Railway | | William IV |
| ? | Tolpuddle Martyrs | | | Poor Law Amendment Act | Robert Peel Prime Minister |
| ? | | Whitworth's screw lathe | 'Railway Mania' | Factory Act | |
| 1846 | ? | | | | Robert Peel resigns |
| ? | | | | Cholera outbreak | Third Chartist Petition |
| ? | | Great Exhibition | | | |
| ? | | | | | Crimean War |
| ? | | Bessemer Converter | | | Treaty of Paris |
| 1865 | | | | | Death of Palmerston |

# 2 Famous people 1700–1900

```
B A K E W E L L H T T B R I N D L E Y
R E D E F O E C H D U D L E Y C E G E
A G D C A I R D T E L F O R D R N I L
Y R W F M A R S H A L L L A M A U L D
B E E R O C K I N G H A M H E W R B E
R M B C O R G N T R O C I A T S B E H
O O B T O N D C U L L E Y N C H W R U
O N T M U L S L E L D E R C A A E T N
K T C O K E L A W O W L L O L Y D T T
W B Y E W M E I K L E A V C F N G A S
I S N B R N D R N L S H D K E O W I M
L T W O R A S S A G T T U E L G O R A
K J S A R K N H P R O R J D S X O O N
I E A B L L E S E Y N J E S S A D E A
N S Y V L K D G O N F E S S I O I B S
S S S E C R E U S M D S S P A L N U M
O O B O I O N R I N E S O P S G Y C Y
N P L A R G U R N E Y O P O P R U K T
T L L E I N N E R V O P N S T I O E H
O B R I D G E W A T E R L E N U R B T
```

**1** Draw five columns in your book like this:

| People associated with agriculture: | People associated with road transport: | People associated with iron and steel: | People associated with canals: | People associated with railways: |
|---|---|---|---|---|
| (Find 7 names) | (Find 6 names) | (Find 9 names) | (Find 6 names) | (Find 2 names) |

**2** Find the following names in the grid on p. 179 and then place them in their appropriate columns.

| | | | | | |
|---|---|---|---|---|---|
| Young | Neilson | Walker | Wilkinson | Dudley | Jessop |
| Marshall | Coke | Brindley | Gilbert | Roebuck | Nasmyth |
| Defoe | Telford | Gurney | Wedgwood | Locke | Hudson |
| Wade | Darby | Meikle | Metcalf | Brunel | Hancock |
| Huntsman | Crawshay | Bakewell | Tull | Bridgewater | Culley |

# 3   Beat the teacher!

This game is for groups of two or three pupils. Follow the instructions below carefully.

**1** Collect a *team letter card* from the teacher and put it on your desk/table.

**2** In your groups of two or three work out ten questions about Social and Economic History using your notebooks and textbooks. Discuss the questions *quietly.* If other groups hear your questions and answers, your team will lose points later on. You will have about 15 minutes on this assignment. Follow the guidelines below:

    **a** Do not make your questions too obscure. ('What colour socks was George Stephenson wearing when he designed the 'Rocket'') or too difficult ('In what year did Richard Trevithick travel to South America?'). If the class decides that your question is too obscure or too difficult, you score zero points for that question.

**b** Make a careful note of the correct answers to your questions.

**3** Each team will take it in turns to ask the class and then the teacher their questions. Teams score one point if no one in the class knows the answer and two points if they *beat the teacher.*

**4** Any team caught cheating loses five points. Any team member who shouts out stupid or silly answers loses his team five points. Team scores will be recorded on the blackboard.

**5** The winning team will be the team with the most points at the end of the game.

# 4 Women in history

**1** Solve the clues to **a–k**. Then find the surnames of the ten famous women in the grid on p. 182.

    **a** She led the Women's Social and Political Union 1903–1914.

    **b** She was Queen of England 1837–1901.

    **c** She became Prime Minister in 1979.

    **d** She threw herself under the King's horse in the 1913 Derby.

    **e** She founded the North London Collegiate School in 1850.

    **f** She discovered radium in 1898.

    **g** She was the first woman doctor to practise in England.

    **h** She flew from Croydon to Australia in 1930.

    **j** She encouraged the match-girls to strike for better conditions in 1888.

    **k** She visited female prisoners in Newgate.

**2** Use a reference book or history textbook to find out one *fact* and one *opinion* about each of the ten famous women listed above. The fact should not be the same as the ten clues above. For example: 'Queen Victoria was married to Prince Albert' is a *fact*, while 'Queen Victoria was England's greatest queen' is an *opinion.*

```
P N O S I V A D Y J
M A R N E W O L R O
A G N I D L E I F H
I Y A K E K O C A N
R L E E H R H T E S
O L P L L U T I H O
T I A N D E R S O N
C H C R A U B S S O
I R E H C T A H T N
V T N A S E B U S S
```

**3** There are also names of nine famous men hidden in the letters on the grid. Who are they and what were they famous for?

# 5  Quiz

Answer these 30 questions about Social and Economic History. All the answers can be found in this book.

**1** Name the village in Nottinghamshire which still uses a system of open field farming.

**2** Who wrote a series of farming reports 1771–1784?

**3** What invention do you associate with John Rastrick?

**4** Who wrote a novel about country life in Oxfordshire called *Lark Rise*?

**5** What was the 'gang system'?

**6** What do the initials WLA stand for?

**7** Who was Daniel Defoe?

**8** When did Abraham Darby move the site of his ironworks to Coalbrookdale?

**9** Which town did the ironmaster Samuel Walker come from?

**10** In coal mining, what are 'spurns' and 'sprogs'?

**11** Who erected a steam engine at Dudley Castle in 1712?

**12** What nickname was given to the building which housed the Great Exhibition of 1851?

**13** Name the machine invented by Henry Bessemer in 1856.

**14** Which textile products do you associate with South Lancashire?

**15** Where did serious turnpike riots take place in 1749?

**16** What term is used to describe the eighteenth century craze for investing in canals?

**17** When was the Birmingham–Worcester Canal opened?

**18** Who or what was *The Graphic*?

**19** Who were the 'Resurrection Men'?

**20** What is a vagrant?

**21** With which aspect of social reform do you associate the name of Elizabeth Fry?

**22** Who were 'Peel's Bloody Gang'?

**23** What was oakum?

**24** Who were the Luddites?

**25** How many 'Tolpuddle Martyrs' were transported to Australia in 1834?

**26** In which city were there serious riots in 1886?

**27** Who was Annie Besant?

**28** Under the terms of the 1834 Poor Law Amendment Act, who were the 'Guardians'?

**29** Who were the 'climbing boys'?

**30** Which killer disease produced serious epidemics in Britain 1831–2, 1838, 1854?

# Crossword

Solve the clues below and then fit them on to the grid. You can find the answers at the back of this book.

## Across

**1** Trade system involving tariffs and regulations (12)

**6** Female sheep (3)

**8** The Duke of Bridgewater's family name (7)

**9** Textile produced mainly in Yorkshire (4)

**10** Pig's stall (3)

**11** French engineer from whom Macadam borrowed road-mending techniques (9)

**14** Prime Minister who repealed the Corn Laws in 1846 (4)

**16** Canal cut by Telford (9)

**18** Iron in its natural state (3)

**20** Capone was a famous American gangster (2)

**21** Doctor of Divinity (2)

**22** In 1731 Jethro Tull wrote 'The _ Horse Hoeing Husbandry' (3)

**24** Slang word for a canal navigator (5)

**26** The royal signature of the King of England 1760–1820 (2)

**28** Initials of country from which we imported most of our raw cotton in 1850 (3)

**29** The practice of giving allowances instead of wages (1795) (12)

**30** The surname of the author of *Self Help* and *Lives of the Great Engineers* (6)

**32** Engineer who built the London to Bristol line (6)

**36** Old word for beer (3)

**37** The period when people invested large sums of money in railways (7,5)

## Down

**2** James Brindley was a civil _____ (8)

**3** Scottish author and philosopher who wrote *Heroes and Hero Worship* (7)

**4** In 1830 the _ Hours Movement was launched by Fielden and Oastler (3)

**5** Surname of man who founded the research centre at Rothamsted (5)

**7** The man who modified and improved the Newcomen steam engine (4)

**10** Before the introduction of canals, most bulky goods were transported by river or _ (3)

**11** Surname of the man who invented the seed drill (4)

**12** Town in Germany (5)

**13** The eighteenth century is sometimes called 'The _ of Reason' (3)

**15** Initials of pressure group dedicated to the abolition of nuclear weapons (3)

**17** Piece of legislation (3)

**19** German socialist and writer, friend of Karl Marx (6)

**21** English Prime Minister 1874–1880 (8)

**23** Old word for 'before' (3)

**25** Carpenter's tool (3)

**27** Two-thirds of the convicts sent to the colonies in 1815–1835 were convicted under the _ Laws (4)

**29** Sub-standard houses (5)

**31** Cast seed (3)

**33** Alcoholic spirit smuggled into England in large quantities in the eighteenth century (3)

**34** Grandmother (3)

**35** Old word for 'meadow' (3)